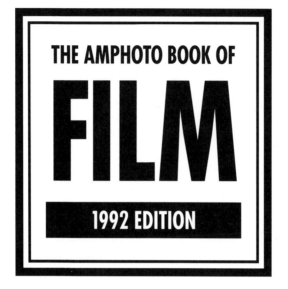

THE AMPHOTO BOOK OF

FILM

1992 EDITION

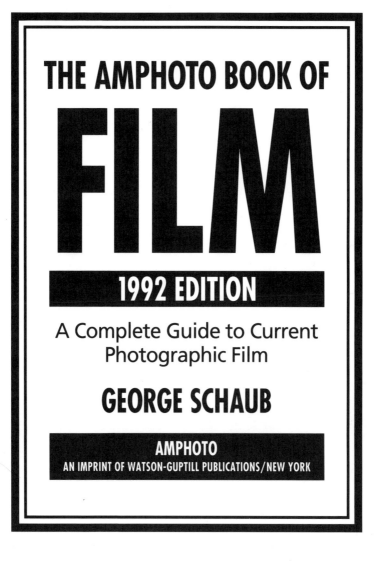

THE AMPHOTO BOOK OF

FILM

1992 EDITION

A Complete Guide to Current Photographic Film

GEORGE SCHAUB

AMPHOTO
AN IMPRINT OF WATSON-GUPTILL PUBLICATIONS/NEW YORK

Editorial concept by Robin Simmen
Designed by Areta Buk
Graphic production by Hector Campbell

Copyright © 1991 by Watson-Guptill Publications, Inc.

First published 1991 in New York by Amphoto,
an imprint of Watson-Guptill Publications, Inc.,
a division of BPI Communications, Inc.,
1515 Broadway, New York, NY 10036

Library of Congress Cataloging-in-Publication Data

Manufactured in the United States of America

1 2 3 4 5 6 7 8 9/99 98 97 96 95 94 93 92 91

CONTENTS

COLOR TRANSPARENCY FILMS

INSTANT BLACK-AND-WHITE PRINT FILMS

LIST OF MANUFACTURERS AND THEIR FILMS

INTRODUCTION

Film technology has undergone a revolution in the past few years. Film manufacturers no longer need to coat actual film emulsions for testing—they now have computer simulation programs that allow them to experiment without the tedious, trial-and-error methods of the past. Once these simulations are complete, they can note the changes in color saturation, grain, and sharpness that result. This has decreased the time it takes to incorporate new technologies in actual products, resulting in the overhaul of virtually every film on the market today. The pace of these developments has been as astounding as the number of new films introduced in a very short period of time.

One major change that has occured within the past few years has been an increase in film speed without a corresponding loss in quality. In the past, slow films were the way to go if a photographer wanted acceptable grain, sharpness, and color rendition. Today, many of the high-speed films offer the quality of slower-speed films of only a few years ago. Perhaps even more important has been the increase in quality—in grain, sharpness, color brilliance, and fidelity—in films of all speeds.

Changes that have been made on a molecular level, including new methods for crystal growth and the incorporation of new color chemistry in film emulsions, have had a profound effect on the ways a film "sees" and what it allows the photographer to record. Exposure latitude—the range of under- and overexposure in which a film delivers an acceptable image—has also been substantially improved. In addition, many films are now of the "boutique" variety. These films are aimed at specific users and applications, and are marketed with a very specific audience in mind. Many offer unique renditions of color, contrast, and color saturation, allowing photographers to make film choice an integral part of the "look" they desire for their images.

Film manufactruers have also begun to engage in a film "newspeak," using techno-jargon to explain the miraculous changes they have made in their products. The following four types of film improvements are highly technical but may be of interest to fim users.

The first involves new crystal constructions. The silver-halide crystals embedded in film are light-responsive, which is what makes capturing images possible. In general, the larger the area of these crystals, the more sensitive the film is to light. The manifestation of these crystals after film development is called "grain," the salt-and-pepper pattern of clumps of crystals and the spaces between them.

New crystal structures—including T-grains and core-shell grains, among others—are more efficient in their light-gathering ability than those of the past. In short, they can match the speed, or light-sensitivity, of larger crystals in past film technology, thus giving greater speed with less grain. The result is faster films with less apparent grain, and slower films with nearly invisible grain. Although the payoff may not be evident in smaller prints, enlargement quickly reveals the quantum leap in quality these new crystal structures offer.

Another area of development has been the trend toward thinner emulsions. When light travels through a material, it has a tendency to be scattered—the thicker the material, the more the dispersion. In some color films, which today sport numerous layers, this could mean less sharp images. Advanced film-coating technology has made a big difference here, allowing film manufacturers to build very sophisticated, multilayered color films without as much concern about its effects on film sharpness.

A third improvement has been the ability to deliver improved color through the refinement of color-coupler technology. During color film processing, the image-forming silver is replaced by color dyes; color couplers are what form the actual dye image. In most color films, color dyes are created during development by color couplers incorporated in the film emulsion itself. Part of this improvement has been the delivery of richer, more saturated colors to new films.

Allied with this technology is the fourth major development, one that affects how cleanly colors reproduce and the way colors interact with one another to capture all the subtle nuances of this colorful world. The use of certain chemical switches—called DIRs and DIARs—helps control these color interactions and also aids in keeping images sharp.

This recent wave of technological developments has produced a virtual golden age of film, and more changes are expected in the near future. In the past five years we've seen quantum leaps in the speed, finer grain, and sharpness of every type and format of film from all manufacturers.

Some of the major products that have emerged include Kodak's T-Max black-and-white films, which offer finer grain than other conventional black-and-white films of similar speed; Kodak Ektar 25 color negative film, arguably the finest-grain color film ever made; Fuji HG 400 Super, a medium-fast color negative film with grain that matches ISO 100 film of the past; and Konica SR-G3200 color negative film, the fastest film available. Other companies have kept pace and made improvements in film stability and overall image quality.

Even so, old favorites still command the loyalty of photographers worldwide. These include the Kodak Kodachrome slide films, first introduced in 1937. Aside from the charm of the Kodachrome rendition, the Kodachrome process has yet to be outdone for long-term image preservation. When stored properly, this unique film-type won't fade, color-shift, or discolor as quickly as other transparency materials. Kodak's Tri-X black-and-white film is still a favorite among shooters, despite the fact that Kodak's T-Max 400 offers finer grain. They like the processing ease and "look" of the older film. And as long as film keeps selling at a certain level, film manufacturers will keep making and marketing it.

As you leaf through this guide, you may notice that the only constant in the film business is change. Very few films appear that were listed in a similar guide published only five years ago. With the current pace of development this phenomenon should continue well into the twenty-first century.

The great variety of films now available represent the film manufacturers' attempts to meet the diverse needs of image makers. Though you might question why a company has twenty slide films, or three varieties of color negative film of the same speed, each product is carefully aimed toward a particular segment of the photography community. While some color-print materials are aimed at amateurs who use the product for nearly every type of shooting situation and lighting condition (correctly or incorrectly), other films are clearly aimed toward professionals who use these products with exacting needs in mind, such as shooting under very specific lighting conditions or when particularly long exposure times are required.

This book will help you wade through all the choices and match the right film to the job at hand. In some cases, choosing one ISO 100 slide film over another is a matter of personal taste; indeed, you may choose one for shooting landscapes and another for portraits, based on how the film renders color saturation or scene contrast.

This guide is a celebration of the film manaufacturers' skills as well as an appraisal of the tools available to photographers. Just as your careful choice of lens, exposure, and point of view contributes to the effectiveness of your images, so does your choice of film. Choosing the right film is crucial to the art of photographic communication.

USING THIS GUIDE

This guide has been set up to make it easy for you to find a film and to quickly identify its characteristics. Overall, the book is divided into four major film categories: color negative films; color transparency films; black-and-white films; and instant films. Film in each category is subdivided by film speed (ISO), then listed in brand-name order. Following the film name are a number of categories that describe that film's characteristics. The categories are:

MANUFACTURER

Each film's manufacturer is listed immediately after the brand name. A list of the full names and addresses of all the film manufacturers referred to appears at the end of the book.

DESIGNATION

This refers to the product code number or a name other than the one in the heading. In some cases, the same type of film may have different codes based upon the format, or film size, in which it is available. For example, Kodak Technical Pan film has product codes of 2415, 4415, and 6415 that identify 35mm, 120, and sheet film products respectively.

Also shown in this category is whether a film has been designated as "Amateur" or "Professional." These designations apparently mean different things to different manufacturers. In many cases, such as with Kodachrome 64, the films are essentially the same, except that the professional product is shipped at the peak of its performance characteristics and is meant to be exposed and processed in a very short period of time. On the other hand, amateur film is shipped at a time when some aging is expected to occur prior to processing and exposure. This aging process takes into account film that may be left in the camera for long periods of time (over a month) and that may not be processed immediately after exposure. Essentially, amateur film is released earlier to allow for the delay between exposure and/or processing, while professional film is fully mature when bought. This maturity means that color balance, speed, and other characteristics are right on target. Also, some professional films are packed with instruction sheets giving tested effective speeds that may be faster or slower than its normal brand film-speed rating, and with information on filter packs for balancing each batch of film.

To keep professional film fresh, you should refrigerate it prior to use (and that goes for dealers as well!) and process it immediately after exposure. Some companies, such as Fuji and Agfa, say that if their professional films are stored under moderate conditions, such refrigeration isn't required due to a special hardening process that maintains color balance and speed at optimum levels. Some photographers refrigerate all professional films regardless of manufacturer.

When professional and amateur products are essentially the same, the professional films in this guide are listed along with their amateur counterparts. This is done to avoid repetition. The listing will appear, for example, as Kodachrome 64 Professional/64 Amateur. In the designation the product codes will show up as KR (Amateur)/PKR (Professional). However, if the two products are substantially different, separate product listings or notes showing the differences are made. (They may be as minor as an extra retouch layer on the base of the film.)

SPEED

This indicates the film speed, or ISO, of the film, which means its relative sensitivity to light. In an elegant arrangement, an ISO 200 film is twice as "fast" as an ISO 100 film and therefore needs one stop less for proper exposure. Thus, an equivalent exposure is obtained at f/11 and 1/125 sec. on an ISO 100 film and f/16 and 1/125 sec. on an ISO 200 film. Choice of film is dependent upon many factors, with speed being one of the most important. In certain instances, choice of film based on speed is a luxury (such as when you can use as low a speed as possible for the finest grain and sharpness); in other instances, it is a necessity (such as when you are shooting in low light, yet want to work with a fairly fast shutter speed). In general, the lower the film speed, the finer the grain and the better the sharpness.

In rare cases, no ISO or a number of ISOs will be shown. This may come up when film speed is dependent upon the light source, developing time, or is determined individually by the manufacturer for each batch of film manufactured. This will be noted accordingly.

BALANCED FOR (COLOR FILMS ONLY)

This refers to the type of light source for which the film has been balanced. Unlike the human brain, film can't adjust to different color temperatures of light. For example, a tungsten-balanced film is manufactured to give correct color balance when exposed under tungsten (3200 degrees Kelvin) light, a light source often used for copy and studio photography. If exposed in daylight (5600 degrees Kelvin), the film will exhibit a decidedly blue cast. Conversely, a daylight-balanced film exposed under artificial light will record with an amber or yellow-red cast in most cases. To a certain extent, when color prints are made from color negative film, this cast can be removed through printer filtration. Color-slide films can be corrected somewhat when duplicate slides are made. However, for the most part, using a film matched to the light source or placing the appropriate color-correcting (CC) filters over the camera lens during exposure yields the best results. Black-and-white film listings don't have a color balance listing, for obvious reasons.

COLOR SENSITIVITY (BLACK-AND-WHITE FILMS ONLY)

Certain colors cause more or less of a reaction in photographic emulsions and, therefore, cause a difference in density and tone reproduction in black-and-white films. These films are divided into five color-sensitivity classes: blue sensitive, orthochromatic, panchromatic, extended-red panchromatic, and infrared. Films in the blue-sensitive class are sensitive only to ultraviolet radiation and blue light. Used mostly in copying and black-and-white transparency work, these high-contrast films can be handled and processed in the darkroom with a safelight.

Orthochromatic films, including some copy films, are sensitive to ultraviolet radiation, blue, and green light but can be processed in red safelight conditions in the darkroom. If used outdoors, this type of film can "block up" the sky in the negative due to the film's over-sensitivity to blue, resulting in a pale or blank sky.

Panchromatic films are used for general photography because they are sensitive to all colors of light plus ultraviolet radiation. These films are best used to give full-tonal-scale renderings of most photographic subjects and are available in the greatest variety of speeds and formats.

Extended-red panchromatic films are more sensitive to red light, which makes these films more effective in reducing haze in photographs of landscapes. They may also be used to reduce the appearance of blemishes in portraits, though they may give flesh tones a somewhat pale or pasty appearance.

Infrared film is sensitive to all wavelengths of light (including ultraviolet) though it does have a higher response at the red/infrared end of the spectrum. This response is enhanced by filtration—use of a deep red or red filter blocks much of the ultraviolet radiation, blue, and green light so that the image is formed by red light and infrared radiation. This makes the film useful for scientific purposes; however, some photographers have seized upon infrared as something of a cult film. Despite the name, infrared film can't be used to detect heat loss from buildings.

RECIPROCITY EFFECT

Exposure times that are longer or shorter than the range for which a film is designed may not provide the optimum exposure and/or color balance for that film. Under these conditions a film may in fact lose sensitivity, and with color films, a color shift can occur. This phenomenon is called the "reciprocity effect." Illumination levels may also influence a film's sensitivity. Manufacturer recommendations for counteracting this effect are included in the listings, along with the exposure times not recommended for use with individual films.

GRAIN

Although attempts have been made recently to quantify this characteristic, grain is essentially a subjective observation of the appearance of the salt-and-pepper pattern of the film's silver crystals or, in color films, the "memory" of those crystals preserved in the dye layers. It may be subjective, but assigning such characteristics as "fine," "extremely fine," or "coarse" allows us to make a relative comparison of grain among films. Naturally, the appearance of grain is also relative to the size enlargement of the image that we observe.

We will not list Diffuse RMS Granularity Values here because scientists are in the midst of resolving the confusion that occurs when measurements between print and slide films are compared. If a new standard is available for the next edition, it will be included in the listings.

DEGREE OF ENLARGEMENT

Photographic film is a very high-quality recording material, but there is a practical limit to which it can be enlarged and still yield a satisfactory image. Given optimum exposure and development, the degree of enlargement possible is a somewhat subjective appraisal of this limit. Of course, any film can be enlarged greatly for special-effects purposes; however, this category in the listings refers to the degree of enlargement for more conventional commercial and pictorial needs. Use this as a comparative measure, rather than a hard-and-fast rule.

RESOLVING POWER

This refers to the ability of a film to distinguish fine detail, which is measured by photographing test targets consisting of series of parallel-line groupings. After exposure and development, the test film is examined through a microscope to determine the smallest set of line pairs that were recorded and can be seen as distinct from one another. The film's resolving power is then stated in terms of lines per millimeter. In general, measurements of resolving power are made at varying exposure levels, with figures given for both high and low levels of light. Naturally, resolving power depends upon the resolution of the camera lens itself, plus correct exposure and development procedures for the film. The figures given are the optimum for each film. The numbers listed in this guide are for the high-contrast image target test alone. The listings can be compared to judge the relative resolving power of each film. In general, those films at 50 lines/mm are regarded as having low resolving power; up to 80 lines/mm are judged medium; up to 125/mm lines are high; up to 200 lines/mm are very high; up to 500 lines/mm are extremely high; and 630 lines/mm or greater have an ultra-high resolving power.

COLOR RENDITION (COLOR FILMS ONLY)

The way a film renders color is an important facet of its personality. Recent films, for example, have been marketed, with "high color saturation." This trend toward high color saturation has not touched all films, as there are many times when photographers want a more neutral color rendition. In addition to overall color richness, some films display a particularly "warm" or "cool" bias; this refers to film that leans toward a slightly yellow or blue take on the world. Though film personality tends to be more important with slide film, a recent group of color print films, the Triade group from Agfa, is marketed on the basis of its degrees of color saturation. The listing for color rendition can be an important one when choosing one brand of similar-speed film over another. The point is that, now more than ever, you have the ability to match film to subject matter based on how you want the color rendered.

EXPOSURE LATITUDE

Given that a film is properly processed, exposure latitude is a general description of the film's ability to deliver usable images when it is either under- or overexposed. Negative materials generally deliver more exposure latitude than transparency materials. In this guide, exposure latitude is expressed in stops or fractions of stops. For example, a certain color negative film may be described as having a +/-2 stop latitude. This means that usable negatives can be obtained if the film is over- or underexposed by 2 stops. Naturally, it is always best to expose properly, but films with greater latitude are more "forgiving" of mistakes. This can be crucial when using films in inexpensive point-and-shoot cameras, or when lighting conditions make it difficult to figure the correct exposure. Using slide film in inexpensive cameras yields unpredictable results, because the less forgiving slide films require more accurate exposure settings than inexpensive cameras usually deliver.

CONTRAST

"Contrast" describes the ability of a film to capture a certain tonal range. The contrast of an image depends on the natural contrast in the scene, plus the effect of exposure and development on the film. For example, if a film is push-processed, contrast will increase; however, if it is normally exposed and developed, the contrast isn't as great. What is described in the listings is the normal contrast of each film. The terms used range from "extremely high" (for certain black-and-white materials used for copying line drawings) to "low." With black-and-white films, contrast can be adjusted according to the developer used and the developing time and temperature. With color film listings, the contrast described is relative to similar color materials.

PROCESSING

This category lists the manufacturer's recommended processing for the film. For color negative films the standard process is called "C-41." For transparency films there are two processes—"E-6" for most films and "K-14" for Kodachrome-type films. Black-and-white films can be processed in a variety of developers for control of contrast and tonal rendition. Listing all the options would be nearly impossible in this guide; therefore, only a few commonly used developers are shown. It is recommended that you refer to the manufacturer's instructions for more extensive information.

PUSH-PROCESSING

Push-processing means extending the film's development to compensate for underexposure. This is useful when the film in your camera can't deliver sufficient speed for the lighting conditions at hand, and/or when you require faster shutter speeds or greater depth of field than the film permits in a particular shooting situation. In addition, many photographers push film to gain a larger grain and/or higher contrast look for graphic or pictorial needs. Until recently, only black-and-white films and E-6 process slide films were considered pushable, but now Kodachrome films and some color negative films are pushed as a normal course of work by some photographers. Push-processing times aren't listed for Kodachrome or color negative films because any push-processing must be done under very strictly controlled laboratory conditions. In addition, Kodachrome films are never processed in home darkrooms.

FORMAT

Different cameras accept different sizes of cassette, roll, and sheet film. This category lists the sizes in which the film is available.

USES

These are recommended uses for the film as defined by its manufacturer. Of course, creative photographers continually find new ways to use materials.

COMMENTS

This section contains miscellaneous information about the film itself—its character, history, or personality. Some of these items are based on the author's experience, others are based on information gleaned from photographers and manufacturers. This category is also a catch-all for any information not contained in the other specifications.

COLOR NEGATIVE FILMS

ISO 25
Ektar 25, Ektar 25 Professional

ISO 50
Agfacolor Ultra 50 Professional

ISO 100
Agfacolor XRG 100
Agfacolor XRS 100 Professional
Ektapress Gold 100
Fujicolor Super HG 100
Fujicolor Reala
Kodacolor Gold 100
Konica Super SR 100
ScotchColor 100
Vericolor HC Professional

ISO 125
Agfacolor Optima 125
Ektar 125

ISO 160
Agfacolor Portrait 160
Fujicolor 160 Professional L
Fujicolor Professional S
Konica Color SR-G 160
Vericolor III Professional

ISO 200
Agfacolor XRG 200
Agfacolor XRS 200 Professional
Fujicolor Super HG 200
Kodacolor Gold 200
Konica Super SR 200
Polaroid Onefilm
ScotchColor 200

ISO 400
Agfacolor XRG 400
Agfacolor XRS 400 Professional
Ektapress Gold 400
Fujicolor Super HG 400
Kodak Gold 400
Konica Super SR 400
ScotchColor 400
Vericolor 400

ISO 1000
Agfacolor XRS 1000 Professional
Ektar 1000

ISO 1600
Ektapress Gold 1600
Fujicolor Super HG 1600
Kodacolor Gold 1600

ISO 3200
Konica SR-G 3200

The vast majority of film shot today is color negative film, with the end product being color prints. In general, today's color negative films offer finer grain, better sharpness, and more true-to-life colors than ever before. In addition, the exposure latitude of most color negative films guarantees more usable pictures per roll than in the past.

Color negative films for general use fall in the ISO 25 to ISO 3200 film-speed range. The former is used when extremely fine-grain and etch-edge sharpness is desired, while the latter allows for color photography under even the dimmest lighting conditions. Between those extremes are films at various speeds. As a rule, for the best possible grain and sharpness, choose the slowest speed film possible. Although an ISO 25 film is superb, there may be times when the lighting conditions preclude its use, and higher film speeds should be chosen.

The overwhelming majority of films in this category are daylight balanced, which means they will deliver correct color balance if exposed outdoors or with electronic flash. A few films for studio use or copy negatives are balanced for other light sources, such as tungsten light. If a color negative film is mismatched with a light source an appropriate color-balancing filter can be used for correction over the camera lens; in addition, some degree of correction can be made when prints are made.

Unlike color transparency film, color negative film has a masking layer that gives it an orange appearance. This can make reading the color of an image in a negative difficult for all but experienced photographers and/or printers. However, this masking layer is a great aid in making prints and is one reason why color negative film usually delivers print quality superior to color transparency film.

A recent trend in color negative film is the availability of customized films for use in very specific shooting situations. For example, Agfa offers a group of three films—Agfacolor Ultra, Optima, and Portrait—under the logo "Triade" whereby each film is touted as having low, medium, and high color saturation. Other companies offer two types of professional film, one with lower contrast than the other: one for portraiture and the other for commercial and industrial photography. In addition, the recent introduction of so-called "premium" films sold in photography stores are films with superior performance characteristics over their amateur counterparts. These premium films straddle the boundary between amateur and professional products, and are marketed toward the so-called "advanced" amateur.

As you look through this section, you'll notice that nearly every manufacturer offers at least one ISO 100, 200, and 400 speed film for amateur use, and as many films for the professional photographer. Choosing one film over another is often a matter of personal taste since each offers a slightly different rendition. Experimentation and testing is the key to finding the film you prefer.

Some of the films here are made for very specific purposes; match the right film to the job at hand to make the job easier. Keep in mind that final results with color negative film are often in the hands of the lab. If you work with the right lab, all these films deliver excellent results. Failure to demand top quality from a lab—in processing, print exposure, and color balance—yields disappointing results from any film.

EKTAR 25, EKTAR 25 PROFESSIONAL

Manufacturer: Eastman Kodak

Designation: Amateur/Professional

Speed: ISO 25

Balanced for: Daylight/electronic flash

Reciprocity effect: No adjustment or filters required in 1/10,000 to 10 second range. Not recommended for exposures longer than 10 seconds.

Grain: Ultra-fine

Degree of enlargement: Extremely high

Resolving power: 200 lines/mm

Color rendition: Rich, saturated colors

Exposure latitude: +2/–1 stop

Contrast: Medium to medium high

Processing: C-41 or equivalent

Push-processing: Not recommended

Format: Amateur, 35mm; Professional, 35mm, 120

Uses: Ektar 25 is excellent for big enlargements of all subject matter.

Comments: This is arguably the finest grain, sharpest color negative film ever produced. Slow speed is the price paid for this, but the results are truly impressive enlargements. Don't use this film with a long lens without a tripod, or in lens/shutter cameras that can't read the ISO 25 DX code. Exposure latitude is less than with conventional color negative films, and contrast is a bit higher than films in the ISO 100 range. Don't compare this film to others in snapshot size; blowups reveal its true beauty. When Kodak made this film available in 120 size, they gave photographers a medium-format film that comes close to current 4 × 5 film in terms of image quality.

**COLOR
NEGATIVE FILMS
ISO 50**

AGFACOLOR ULTRA 50 PROFESSIONAL

Manufacturer: Agfa

Designation: Professional

Speed: ISO 50

Balanced for: Daylight/electronic flash

Reciprocity effect: No compensation is required for exposures between 1/10,000 and 1/2 sec.; add 1 stop for a 1 second exposure; add 2 stops for a 10 second exposure; add 3 stops for a 100 second exposure.

Grain: Very fine

Degree of enlargement: Very high

Resolving power: 140 lines/mm

Color rendition: Rich, saturated colors

Exposure latitude: +2/–2 stops

Contrast: Medium to medium high

Processing: C-41 or equivalent

Push-processing: Not recommended

Format: 35mm, 120

Uses: A professional color print film designed to deliver a high color saturation print for landscapes, commercial work, and other professional uses. Also used as a premium film for advanced amateurs.

Comments: Ultra 50 is part of the Agfa Triade of negative films that offers various degrees of color saturation. This is the slowest and most color saturated of the three. Colors are truly rich, with bright, clean yellows, deep yet open reds, and dazzling blues. Slight overexposure seems to add to the color-saturated effect.

AGFACOLOR XRG 100

Manufacturer: Agfa

Designation: Amateur

Speed: ISO 100

Balanced for: Daylight/electronic flash

Reciprocity effect: No compensation is required for exposures in 1/10,000 to 1/2 sec. range. For exposures of 1 second add 1/2 stop; for 10 second exposures, add 2 stops; for 100 second exposures, add 3 stops.

Grain: Very fine

Degree of enlargement: High

Resolving power: Not available

Color rendition: Rich, saturated colors

Exposure latitude: +/–2 stops

Contrast: Medium

Processing: C-41 or equivalent

Push-processing: Not recommended

Format: 35mm

Uses: A general-purpose color negative film for prints and enlargements.

Comments: Agfa has produced a very fine-grain, sharp, and color-saturated print film. The real speed of this film is ISO 160, even though it is DX-coded for ISO 100. It has been rated slower to take advantage of the finer grain and exposure latitude that slight overexposure affords. This makes it a good choice for lens/shutter cameras, whose built-in meters aren't always accurate. Many other film manufacturers rate their amateur film slower; however, Agfa's film is of note because it is the fastest with an ISO 100 rating.

**COLOR
NEGATIVE FILMS**

ISO 100

AGFACOLOR XRS 100 PROFESSIONAL

Manufacturer: Agfa

Designation: Professional

Speed: ISO 100

Balanced for: Daylight/electronic flash

Reciprocity effect: For exposures in 1/10,000 to 1/2 sec. range, no compensation is required. Add 1/2 stop for a 1 second exposure; add 2 stops for a 10 second exposure; add 3 stops for a 100 second exposure.

Grain: Very fine

Degree of enlargement: Very high

Resolving power: Not available

Color rendition: Rich, saturated colors

Exposure latitude: +2/–1 stop

Contrast: Medium

Processing: C-41 or equivalent

Push-processing: Not recommended

Format: 35mm, 120, 4 × 5, 8 × 10

Uses: A professional-quality color negative film for fashion, studio, and location photography.

Comments: This update on the Agfa professional line offers much richer colors than past products, plus gives increased sharpness and a somewhat finer grain.

EKTAPRESS GOLD 100

Manufacturer: Eastman Kodak

Designation: 5115, Professional

Speed: ISO 100

Balanced for: Daylight/electronic flash

Reciprocity effect: No compensation is required when exposures are made in the 1/10,000 to 1/10 sec. range. For 1 second exposure, add 1 stop and a 20Y filter. Not recommended for exposures longer than 1 second.

Grain: Very fine

Degree of enlargement: High

Resolving power: 100 lines/mm

Color rendition: Rich colors, neutral

Exposure latitude: +2 1/2/–1 1/2 stop

Contrast: Medium

Processing: C-41 or equivalent

Format: 35mm

Push-processing: Not recommended

Uses: Provides maximum image quality under relatively bright daylight and flash exposure conditions.

Comments: Ektapress Gold 100 is the slowest speed member of the Ektapress family. It offers very fine grain, good sharpness, and a high degree of enlargement. It is sold without an outer wrapper in boxes of 5 or 50 cannisters and is intended for photojournalists and other photographers who use large amounts of film in situations that prohibit refrigerated storage.

**COLOR
NEGATIVE FILMS
ISO 100**

FUJICOLOR SUPER HG 100

Manufacturer: Fuji

Designation: CN, Amateur

Speed: ISO 100

Balanced for: Daylight/electronic flash

Reciprocity effect: For exposures in 1/10,000 to 1/10 sec. range, no compensation is needed. For exposures of 1 second, add 1/2 stop; for 10 second exposures, add 1 stop; for 100 second exposures, add 2 stops.

Grain: Very fine

Degree of enlargement: Very high

Resolving power: 125 lines/mm

Color rendition: Rich, saturated colors

Exposure latitude: +2/−1½ stops

Contrast: Medium

Processing: C-41 or equivalent

Push-processing: Not recommended

Format: 110, 126, 35mm, 120

Uses: A general-purpose color negative film for amateurs

Comments: This revision of the Fujicolor ISO 100 color negative entry offers improved flesh-tone rendition and color purity. Exposure latitude is also improved, which is a bonus for lens/shutter 35mm users who don't have meticulously calibrated cameras. This film is also designed to improve the quality of flash pictures, another boon for snapshot camera users. A very good all-purpose amateur color negative film.

FUJICOLOR REALA

Manufacturer: Fuji

Designation: CS, Amateur/Professional

Speed: ISO 100

Balanced for: Daylight/electronic flash

Reciprocity effect: No compensation required for exposures between 1/10,000 and 1/10 sec. For 1 second exposure, add 1/2 stop; for 10 second exposure, add 1 stop; for 100 second exposure, add 2 stops.

Grain: Very fine

Degree of enlargement: Very high

Resolving power: 125 lines/mm

Color rendition: Rich, natural colors

Exposure latitude: +2/–1 stop

Contrast: Medium

Processing: C-41 or equivalent

Push-processing: Not recommended

Format: 35mm, 120, 220

Uses: A general-purpose color negative film for amateurs, advanced amateurs, and professionals.

Comments: In addition to conventional emulsion layers, Reala has a fourth type of cyan-sensitive layer that Fuji claims allows a response to light similar to human vision. The practical effect of this very complex system is that Reala yields true colors under a wide variety of lighting conditions. This is most apparent under fluorescent lighting, possibly the worst light source for pleasing color photography. Fuji claims that prints made from Reala negatives shot under fluorescent conditions require less filtration for good color than do other color negative films. In addition, Reala does an excellent job with pastels and subtle nuances of color, and provides superb highlight-to-shadow gradation.

KODACOLOR GOLD 100

Manufacturer: Eastman Kodak

Designation: CA, Amateur

Speed: ISO 100

Balanced for: Daylight/electronic flash

Reciprocity effect: Recommended exposure is between 1/10,000 and 1/10 sec. For a 1 second exposure, add 1 stop and a CC20Y filter. Not recommended for exposures longer than 1 second.

Grain: Very fine

Degree of enlargement: High

Resolving power: 100 lines/mm

Color rendition: Rich, saturated colors

Exposure latitude: +2 1/2/−1 1/2 stop

Contrast: Medium

Processing: C-41 or equivalent

Push-processing: Not recommended

Format: 35mm, 120

Uses: General-purpose film excellent for amateur photography of all sorts. The 120 format has two-sided retouching surface.

Comments: This replaces Kodak VR-G100 film with more pleasing flesh tones. Kodacolor Gold 100 has high sharpness, good color saturation, a wide exposure latitude that forgives exposure errors, and provides very good color accuracy. The 120 version is suited for old amateur roll-film cameras, although it is also used for wedding and portrait work where rich color saturation is needed. Overalll, it is an excellent all-purpose amateur color negative film.

KONICA SUPER SR 100

Manufacturer: Konica

Designation: Amateur

Speed: ISO 100

Balanced for: Daylight/electronic flash

Reciprocity effect: No compensation required for exposures in 1/10,000 to 1 second range. Add 1 stop and a 10M filter for 10 second exposures. Not recommended for exposures beyond 10 seconds.

Grain: Very fine

Degree of enlargement: High

Resolving power: 100 lines/mm

Color rendition: Rich colors

Exposure latitude: +2/–1 stop

Contrast: Medium

Processing: C-41 or equivalent

Push-processing: Not recommended

Format: 35mm, 120

Uses: A general-purpose amateur color negative film. Very fine grain and excellent sharpness allow for big enlargements.

Comments: Konica technology has produced an excellent color negative film with crisp and vivid color rendition. This film is formulated to produce excellent results with a flash and is a very good all-purpose amateur color negative film.

SCOTCHCOLOR 100

Manufacturer: 3M

Designation: Amateur

Speed: ISO 100

Balanced for: Daylight/electronic flash

Reciprocity effect: For exposures in 1/10,000 to 1 second range, no compensation is required. For a 10 second exposure, add 1/3 stop and a CC5Y filter; for a 100 second exposure, add 1 stop and a CC10Y filter.

Grain: Fine

Degree of enlargement: High

Resolving power: 100 lines/mm

Color rendition: Rich colors

Exposure latitude: +2/–1 stop

Contrast: Medium

Processing: C-41 or equivalent

Push-processing: Not recommended

Format: 35mm

Uses: An amateur color-print film for general photography.

Comments: This upgrade of ScotchColor 100 offers improved image stability, wider exposure latitude, and higher color saturation than its predecessor.

VERICOLOR HC PROFESSIONAL

Manufacturer: Eastman Kodak

Designation: 6329 (120); 4329 (sheet film); Professional

Speed: ISO 100

Balanced for: Daylight/electronic flash

Reciprocity effect: No compensation required for exposures in 1/10,000 to 1/10 sec. range; for a 1 second exposure, add 1 stop and a 20Y filter. Not recommended for exposures longer than 1 second.

Grain: Very fine

Degree of enlargement: High

Resolving power: 100 lines/mm

Color rendition: Rich, saturated colors

Exposure latitude: +2/–1 stops

Contrast: Moderately high

Processing: C-41 or equivalent

Push-processing: Not recommended

Format: 120, 4 × 5, 8 × 10

Uses: Commercial, industrial, low-level aerial, environmental portraiture, and other professional applications that call for increased color saturation.

Comments: This professional film from Kodak is an alternative to the more neutral colors of Vericolor III and offers higher color saturation and a bit more contrast. In certain commercial applications, these characteristics add to the impact of an image. This film also works well outdoors under low-contrast lighting conditions, such as on cloudy days or in deep shade.

**COLOR
NEGATIVE FILMS
ISO 125**

AGFACOLOR
OPTIMA 125

Manufacturer: Agfa

Designation: Professional

Speed: ISO 125

Balanced for: Daylight/electronic flash

Reciprocity effect: No compensation is required for exposures in 1/10,000 to 1/2 sec. range. For a 1 second exposure, add 1 stop; add 2 stops for a 10 second exposure; add 3 stops for a 100 second exposure.

Grain: Very fine

Degree of enlargement: Very high

Resolving power: 150 lines/mm

Color rendition: Rich, neutral colors

Exposure latitude: +/–2 stops

Contrast: Medium

Processing: C-41 or equivalent

Push-processing: Not recommended

Format: 35mm, 120, 4 × 5, 8 × 10

Uses: A medium-speed, professional color-print film for landscapes, portraits, and general-purpose professional and advanced amateur photography.

Comments: Optima is part of the Agfa Triade of color negative films, positioned in the middle of the color-saturation pack. Colors are rich and neutral, plus the film has excellent exposure latitude.

EKTAR 125

Manufacturer: Eastman Kodak

Designation: Amateur

Speed: ISO 125

Balanced for: Daylight/electronic flash

Reciprocity effect: No compensation required for exposures in 1/10,000 to 1 second range. For a 10 second exposure, add 1 stop and CC20Y filter. Not recommended for exposures longer than 10 seconds.

Grain: Very fine

Degree of enlargement: Very high

Resolving power: 160 lines per/mm

Color rendition: Rich, saturated colors

Exposure latitude: +2/−1 1/2 stops

Contrast: Medium

Processing: C-41 or equivalent

Push-processing: Not recommended

Format: 35mm

Uses: A premium color negative film for general-purpose photography.

Comments: Ektar 125 is a premium color negative film that can be used in both SLR and lens/shutter 35mm cameras. Although most lens/shutter cameras with a DX coding of ISO 125 default to ISO 100, that does not present an exposure problem with this film. Ektar 125 has over two stops more speed than Ektar 25, another premium Kodak color negative film. The wide exposure latitude, extremely fine grain, and excellent sharpness make this a good choice for advanced amateurs who want high-quality images.

AGFACOLOR PORTRAIT 160

Manufacturer: Agfa

Designation: Professional

Speed: ISO 160

Balanced for: Daylight/electronic flash

Reciprocity effect: No compensation is required for exposures in 1/10,000 to 1/2 sec. range. Add 1/2 stop for a 1 second exposure; add 2 stops for a 10 second exposure; add 3 stops for a 100 second exposure.

Grain: Very fine

Degree of enlargement: High

Resolving power: 150 lines/mm

Color rendition: Rich, neutral colors

Exposure latitude: +2/–1 1/2 stops

Contrast: Medium

Processing: C-41 or equivalent

Push-processing: Not recommended

Format: 35mm, 120

Uses: A neutral, somewhat low color-saturation film ideal for portraits, landscapes, and general professional and advanced amateur photography.

Comments: As part of the Agfa Triade marketing scheme, Portrait 160 is the lowest color-saturation film of the three. As such, it is a very good choice for portraiture or when a lower saturation rendition of scenes is desired. Grain and sharpness are excellent for the speed.

FUJICOLOR 160
PROFESSIONAL L

Manufacturer: Fuji

Designation: NLP, Professional

Speed: ISO 160

Balanced for: Tungsten light/3200K

Reciprocity effect: Designed for best results with shutter speeds of 1/30 to 1 second. For exposures of 2 seconds, increase exposure by 1/2 stop; for 8 second exposures, increase exposure 1 stop; for 64 second exposures, add 1 1/2 stops. For daylight use, add 85B filter, and rate on handheld meter at EI 100.

Grain: Very fine

Degree of enlargement: High

Resolving power: 100 lines/mm

Color rendition: Neutral, true colors

Exposure latitude: +2/–1 stop

Contrast: Medium

Processing: C-41 or equivalent

Push-processing: Not recommended

Format: 120, 4 × 5, 8 × 10

Uses: For product, copy, advertising, illustration, and architectural work where long exposures under tungsten light are required.

Comments: This film has been specially formulated to handle the color problems often inherent to long exposure times such as shifting and crossovers. Its broad exposure latitude is helpful when lighting conditions are difficult.

COLOR NEGATIVE FILMS

ISO 160

FUJICOLOR PROFESSIONAL S

Manufacturer: Fuji

Designation: NSP, Professional

Speed: ISO 160

Balanced for: Daylight/electronic flash

Reciprocity effect: No compensation required when exposed at 1/10,000 to 1/4 sec. Add 1/2 stop for 1 second exposures. Not recommended for exposures longer than 1 second.

Grain: Very fine

Degree of enlargement: High

Resolving power: 113 lines/mm

Color rendition: Rich, natural colors

Exposure latitude: +2/–1 stops

Contrast: Medium

Processing: C-41 or equivalent

Push-processing: Not recommended

Format: 120, 4 × 5, 8 × 10

Uses: Designed for commercial, fashion, and other professional work with shutter speeds of 1/15 sec. or faster.

Comments: Fuji's grain technology has produced a film with a speed of ISO 160 and grain comparable to lower-speed films. The film yields rich, faithful color reproduction and wide highlight-to-shadow gradation. Though its specifications provide for slow shutter speeds, best results are obtained when this film is exposed at 1/15 sec. and faster.

KONICA COLOR SR-G 160

Manufacturer: Konica

Designation: Professional

Speed: ISO 160

Balanced for: Daylight/electronic flash

Reciprocity effect: Designed for exposures between 1/10 and 1/10,000 sec.

Grain: Very fine

Degree of enlargement: High

Resolving power: 100 lines/mm

Color rendition: Rich, natural colors

Exposure latitude: +2/–1 stop

Contrast: Medium

Processing: C-41 or equivalent

Push-processing: Not recommended

Format: 35mm, 120, long rolls (100 ft.): 35mm, 46mm, 70mm

Uses: A professional film for portraits, weddings, and other studio work.

Comments: This very pleasing portrait film has excellent sharpness and grain for enlargements. Contrast is medium, with excellent flesh tones and a soft and delicate gradation from highlights through shadows. Color rendition is natural and pleasing, which makes it a favorite of portrait photographers.

COLOR NEGATIVE FILMS

ISO 160

VERICOLOR III PROFESSIONAL

Manufacturer: Eastman Kodak

Designation: 6006 (120/220); 5026 (35mm, 35mm roll, 46mm roll, 70mm roll); 4106 (sheet film); Professional.

Speed: ISO 160

Balanced for: Daylight/electronic flash

Reciprocity effect: No compensation required for exposures in 1/10,000 to 1/10 sec. range. Not recommended for exposures of 1 second or longer.

Grain: Very fine

Degree of enlargement: High

Resolving power: 100 lines/mm

Color rendition: Rich, neutral colors

Exposure latitude: +2/–1 stop

Contrast: Medium

Processing: C-41 or equivalent

Push-processing: Not recommended

Format: 35mm, 120, 220, long rolls (100 ft.): 35mm, 46mm, 70mm; 4 × 5, 5 × 7, 8 × 10

Uses: A professional color negative film for wedding, portrait, and general commercial photography.

Comments: Long known as the standard for wedding and portrait photographers, Vericolor III delivers excellent flesh-tone reproduction, excellent tonal reproduction, and rich neutral colors. It is available in virtually every conventional format and, thus, can be used with familiarity in the studio and in the field. It is also one film that virtually every professional lab knows how to handle. Vericolor III offers very fine grain for the speed.

AGFACOLOR XRG 200

Manufacturer: Agfa

Designation: Amateur

Speed: ISO 200

Balanced for: Daylight/electronic flash

Reciprocity effect: No compensation is required for exposures in 1/10,000 to 1/2 sec. range. For a 1 second exposure, add 1 stop; for a 10 second exposure, add 2 stops; for a 100 second exposure, add 3 stops.

Grain: Fine

Degree of enlargement: High

Resolving power: Not available

Color rendition: Rich, saturated colors

Exposure latitude: +2/–1 stop

Contrast: Medium

Processing: C-41 or equivalent

Push-processing: Not recommended

Format: 110, 126, 35mm, Rapid 35 (a discontinued Agfa camera cassette)

Uses: A general-purpose color negative film for prints and enlargements.

Comments: This medium-fast-speed color negative film has fine grain for the speed, good sharpness, and wide exposure latitude. It can be used for exposures in fairly dim light as well as bright light outdoors.

AGFACOLOR XRS 200 PROFESSIONAL

Manufacturer: Agfa

Designation: Professional

Speed: ISO 200

Balanced for: Daylight/electronic flash

Reciprocity effect: No compensation required for exposures in 1/10,000 to 1/2 sec. range. For a 1 second exposure, add 1 stop; for a 10 second exposure, add 2 stops; for a 100 second exposure, add 3 stops.

Grain: Fine

Degree of enlargement: High

Resolving power: Not available

Color rendition: Rich, saturated colors

Exposure latitude: +2/−1 1/2 stops

Contrast: Medium

Processing: C-41 or equivalent

Push-processing: Not recommended

Format: 35mm, 120

Uses: A medium-fast professional color negative film for general use.

Comments: A very sharp, fine-grain color print film for use when lighting conditions require slightly more speed than ISO 100 film delivers. It is very effective with subtle colors and lends itself to excellent shadow to highlight separation.

FUJICOLOR SUPER HG 200

Manufacturer: Fuji

Designation: Amateur

Speed: ISO 200

Balanced for: Daylight/electronic flash

Reciprocity effect: No compensation required for exposures in range of 1/10,000 to 1/10 sec. For a 1 second exposure, add 1/2 stop; for a 10 second exposure, add 1 stop; for a 100 second exposure, add 2 stops.

Grain: Fine

Degree of enlargement: High

Resolving power: 100 lines/mm

Color rendition: Rich, saturated colors

Exposure latitude: +2/−1 stop

Contrast: Medium

Processing: C-41 or equivalent

Push-processing: Not recommended

Format: 35mm

Uses: A general-purpose medium-speed film for moderately low-light and daylight/flash photography.

Comments: Many consider the ISO 200 speed ideal for all-around shooting. It can be used in some low-light situations and extends the flash range beyond that offered by using ISO 100 film. This Fuji film comes with excellent image quality, good grain, and excellent sharpness.

KODACOLOR GOLD 200

Manufacturer: Eastman Kodak

Designation: CB, Amateur

Speed: ISO 200

Balanced for: Daylight/electronic flash

Reciprocity effect: Recommended exposure is between 1/10,000 and 1/10 sec. For a 1 second exposure, add 1 stop and CC20Y filter. Not recommended for exposures longer than 1 second.

Grain: Fine

Degree of enlargement: High

Resolving power: 100 lines/mm

Color rendition: Rich, saturated colors

Exposure latitude: +2 1/2/−1 stop

Contrast: Medium

Processing: C-41 or equivalent

Push-processing: Not recommended

Format: 110, 126, 35mm

Uses: A very good general-purpose amateur color negative film.

Comments: This film bridges the gap between the higher quality but lower speed of ISO 100 color-print films and the somewhat grainier, but faster ISO 400 color print film for general picture taking. Recommended for use with compact 35mm cameras. Its speed/quality balance offers the greatest shooting leeway. Knowledgeable amateurs consider this the "universal" speed for snapshot photography, and this is one of the best-selling films in this class.

KONICA SUPER SR 200

Manufacturer: Konica

Designation: Amateur

Speed: ISO 200

Balanced for: Daylight/electronic flash

Reciprocity effect: No adjustments required for exposures in 1/10,000 to 1 second range. Add 1 stop for 10 second exposure.

Grain: Fine

Degree of enlargement: High

Resolving power: 100 lines/mm

Color rendition: Rich, neutral colors

Exposure latitude: +2/–1 stop

Contrast: Medium

Processing: C-41 or equivalent

Push processing: Not recommended

Format: Disc, 110, 126, 35mm

Uses: A very fine-grain, sharp, low-to-medium contrast color negative film for general-purpose photography.

Comments: Konica technology has produced a very impressive medium-fast film that has a slightly lower contrast than other films in this speed class. As such, it is a good choice for portraits and scenes where subtle gradation of tones is desired.

COLOR NEGATIVE FILMS

ISO 200

POLAROID ONEFILM

Manufacturer: Polaroid/3M

Designation: Amateur

Speed: ISO 200

Balanced for: Daylight/electronic flash

Reciprocity effect: No compensation required for exposures in 1/10,000 to 1 second range. Add 1/3 stop for a 10 second exposure; add 1 1/2 stops and 10Y and 10G filter for a 100 second exposure.

Grain: Fine

Degree of enlargement: Moderately high

Resolving power: 98 lines/mm

Color rendition: Rich colors

Exposure latitude: +2/–1 stop

Contrast: Medium

Processing: C-41 or equivalent

Push-processing: Not recommended

Format: Disc, 110, 126, 35mm

Uses: A general-purpose, amateur color negative film.

Comments: Polaroid has marketed this film as a universal print film that can handle a wide variety of amateur picture-taking needs. Within the scope of what an ISO 200 color negative film can do, these claims are true. However, no single film is right for every picture.

SCOTCHCOLOR 200

Manufacturer: 3M

Designation: Amateur

Speed: ISO 200

Balanced for: Daylight/electronic flash

Reciprocity effect: For exposures in 1/10,000 to 1 second range no compensation is required. Add 1/3 stop for a 10 second exposure; add 1 1/2 stops and a 10G and 10Y filter for 100 second exposures.

Grain: Fine

Degree of enlargement: Moderately high

Resolving power: 98 lines/mm

Color rendition: Rich colors

Exposure latitude: +2/–1 stop

Contrast: Medium

Processing: C-41 or equivalent

Push-processing: Not recommended

Format: 35mm

Uses: A general-purpose, amateur color negative film.

Comments: Scotch has upgraded its color negative film lineup. This film has improved exposure latitude, sharpness, and grain, plus it offers richer colors than the Scotch films of the past. In addition, this film has been made with improved printing compatible with Kodacolor films, a plus for those who have films processed in minilabs and wholesale lab operations.

AGFACOLOR XRG 400

Manufacturer: Agfa

Designation: Amateur

Speed: ISO 400

Balanced for: Daylight/electronic flash

Reciprocity effect: No compensation is required for exposures in 1/10,000 to 1/2 sec. range. For a 1 second exposure, add 1 stop; for a 10 second exposure, add 2 stops; for a 100 second exposure, add 3 stops.

Grain: Moderate

Degree of enlargement: Moderately high

Resolving power: Not available

Color rendition: Rich, saturated colors

Exposure latitude: +2/−1 stop

Contrast: Medium/medium high

Processing: C-41 or equivalent

Push-processing: Not recommended

Format: 35mm

Uses: A general-purpose fast color negative film.

Comments: This fast film from Agfa offers moderately fine grain, very rich colors, and good exposure latitude, and it performs well in low light.

AGFACOLOR XRS 400 PROFESSIONAL

Manufacturer: Agfa

Designation: Professional

Speed: ISO 400

Balanced for: Daylight/electronic flash

Reciprocity effect: For exposures in 1/10,000 to 1/2 sec. range no compensation is required. Add 1 stop for a 1 second exposure; add 2 stops for a 10 second exposure; add 3 stops for a 100 second exposure.

Grain: Moderately fine

Degree of enlargement: Moderately high

Resolving power: Not available

Color rendition: Rich, saturated colors

Exposure latitude: +2/–1 ½ stops

Contrast: Medium

Processing: C-41 or equivalent

Push-processing: Not recommended

Format: 35mm, 120

Uses: A fast, professional color print film for use with candids and when light is low or increased shutter speed and/or depth of field is required.

Comments: This fast film offers fine grain and excellent sharpness for its speed, plus excellent tonal gradation in highlight and shadows. Colors are richer and more saturated than with the previous Agfa professional line. Good exposure latitude makes this film useful when lighting conditions are difficult or when exact exposure is difficult to determine.

EKTAPRESS GOLD 400

Manufacturer: Eastman Kodak

Designation: 5113, Professional

Speed: ISO 400

Balanced for: Daylight/electronic flash

Reciprocity effect: No compensation is required for exposures in 1/10,000 to 1/10 sec. range. Add 1/3 stop for a 1 second exposure; add 1 stop for a 10 second exposure. Not recommended for exposures longer than 10 seconds.

Grain: Fine

Degree of enlargement: Moderately high

Resolving power: 100 lines/mm

Color rendition: Rich, neutral colors

Exposure latitude: +2/–1 stop

Contrast: Medium

Processing: C-41 or equivalent

Push-processing: Add 30 seconds developing time for EI 800; add 1 minute for EI 1600.

Format: 35mm

Uses: A medium-fast film for low-light and action photography that can be pushed up to 2 stops when necessary.

Comments: This film was designed for press photographers. When the light is low and/or the action fast, this professional film offers good grain and sharpness for the speed, plus the flexibility of push-processing when needed. This and other Ektapress films have professional tolerances but don't need refrigerated storage to maintain their status. It is DX-coded, so be sure to override the automatic speed setting when pushing.

FUJICOLOR SUPER HG 400

Manufacturer: Fuji

Designation: Amateur

Speed: ISO 400

Balanced for: Daylight/electronic flash

Reciprocity effect: Exposures can be made from 1/10,000 to 1/10 sec. without filter or exposure compensation. Add 1/2 stop for 1 a second exposure; 1 1/2 stops for a 10 second exposure; 2 1/2 stops for a 100 second exposure.

Grain: Very fine for the speed

Degree of enlargement: Moderately high

Resolving power: 100 lines/mm

Color rendition: Rich, saturated colors

Exposure latitude: +/−2 stops

Contrast: Medium

Processing: C-41 or equivalent

Push-processing: Not recommended

Format: 35mm, 120

Uses: A fast, fine-grain color negative film for daylight as well as low-light photography.

Comments: This breakthrough fast film offers grain comparable to ISO 100 film of a few years past. Its colors are rich and saturated, with slightly warm flesh tones and excellent sharpness for the speed. It is good for extending the flash range in lens/shutter cameras. Enlargements reveal excellent grain structure.

KODAK GOLD 400

Manufacturer: Eastman Kodak

Designation: Amateur

Speed: ISO 400

Balanced for: Daylight/electronic flash

Reciprocity effect: Exposures can be made from 1/10,000 to 10 seconds without filter or exposure change. Not recommended for exposures longer than 10 seconds.

Grain: Very fine for the speed

Degree of enlargement: Moderately high

Resolving power: 100 lines/mm

Color rendition: Rich, saturated colors

Exposure latitude: +3/–2 stop

Contrast: Medium

Processing: C-41 or equivalent

Push-processing: Not recommended

Format: 110, 35mm

Uses: This general-purpose film can be used in all lighting conditions, but it is especially suited for low-light shooting or when the flash range must be extended beyond that available with slower film.

Comments: This recent upgrade and replacement of Kodacolor Gold 400 film offers better color rendition when flash is used, an expanded exposure latitude, and better latent image keeping stability (film kept in the camera for a long time after partial exposure of roll maintains its image quality). Improved 400 speed amateur film from Kodak contains T-grain emulsion technology, which yields very fine grain for the speed. Rich colors are an added bonus.

KONICA SUPER SR 400

Manufacturer: Konica

Designation: Amateur

Speed: ISO 400

Balanced for: Daylight/electronic flash

Reciprocity effect: No adjustments required for exposures in 1/10,00 to 1 second range. Add 1 stop and CC10M filter for a 10 second exposure.

Grain: Very fine for speed

Degree of enlargement: Moderate

Resolving power: 100 lines/mm

Color rendition: Rich, saturated colors

Exposure latitude: +2/–1 stop

Contrast: Medium

Processing: C-41 or equivalent

Push-processing: Not recommended

Format: 110, 35mm, 120

Uses: A medium-fast color negative film for general picture-taking, especially suited for low-light conditions. Also used as a daylight film with telephoto lenses or when a fast shutter speed and/or narrow aperture is required.

Comments: This revision of Konica's ISO 400 color negative film is very sharp and has fine grain for a fast film. Colors are very rich, with subtle tonal reproduction. While designed for daylight/electronic flash exposure, this film will yield good results under artificial light, with color balancing further enhanced during printing. New technology is claimed to reduce the degree of color filtration when film is exposed under fluorescent lighting without flash.

SCOTCHCOLOR 400

Manufacturer: 3M

Designation: Amateur

Speed: ISO 400

Balanced for: Daylight/electronic flash

Reciprocity effect: No exposure compensation is required for exposures from 1/10,000 to 10 seconds; add 1 stop and a CC20Y filter for exposures of 100 seconds.

Grain: Medium

Degree of enlargement: Moderately high

Resolving power: 85 lines/mm

Color rendition: Rich colors

Exposure latitude: +2 1/2/–1 1/2 stop

Contrast: Medium to medium high

Processing: C-41 or equivalent

Push-processing: Not recommended

Format: 35mm

Uses: A general-purpose amateur color negative film.

Comments: Scotch has worked hard to create a competitive ISO 400 color negative film. Recent improvements include a modified UV-filtering layer in the emulsion to improve color reproduction and reduce excess bluishness in open shade and distant scenics, plus improved stability in unexposed and exposed film. Scotchcolor is generally available at a lower price than its main competition and may represent a good value for those who do a lot of shooting.

VERICOLOR 400

Manufacturer: Eastman Kodak

Designation: VPH, Professional; 6028 (120/220); 5028 (35mm, 46mm); 4028 (sheet film).

Speed: ISO 400

Balanced for: Daylight/electronic flash

Reciprocity effect: No compensation is required for exposures in 1/10,000 to 1/30 sec. range. No recommendations for longer exposures than those listed above.

Grain: Fine

Degree of enlargement: Moderately high

Resolving power: 100 lines/mm

Color rendition: Rich, neutral colors

Exposure latitude: +2/−1 stop

Contrast: Medium

Processing: C-41 or equivalent

Push-processing: Not recommended

Format: 35mm, 35mm and 46mm long roll, 120, 220, 4 × 5, 8 × 10

Uses: Commercial, industrial, environmental, portraits, and candid wedding photography.

Comments: This professional film incorporates T-grains, which results in a relatively fine grain for the speed. Although critical control under artificial light requires the use of color-balancing filters, it can be exposed in most existing light conditions without filters, and balanced during printing. Many wedding photographers use this film for candid work in churches and synagogues where flash is prohibited. Film retouching can be done on either the base or emulsion side.

COLOR NEGATIVE FILMS

ISO 1000

AGFACOLOR XRS 1000 PROFESSIONAL

Manufacturer: Agfa

Designation: Professional

Speed: ISO 1000

Balanced for: Daylight/electronic flash

Reciprocity effect: No compensation is required for exposures in 1/10,000 to 1/2 sec. range. Add 1/2 stop for a 1 second exposure; 2 stops for a 10 second exposure; 3 stops for a 100 second exposure.

Grain: Moderate

Degree of enlargement: Moderately low

Resolving power: Not available

Color rendition: Neutral colors

Exposure latitude: +2/–1 stop

Contrast: Medium

Processing: C-41 or equivalent

Push-processing: Not recommended

Format: 35mm, 120

Uses: A fast color negative film for low-light photography.

Comments: This fast film delivers moderately fine grain and good sharpness for its speed. Though the film is balanced for daylight/electronic flash, it is put to best use in extremely low light or under artificial light. Photos made in bright daylight may suffer from too much contrast.

EKTAR 1000

Manufacturer: Eastman Kodak

Designation: Amateur

Speed: ISO 1000

Balanced for: Daylight/electronic flash

Reciprocity effect: No adjustments necessary for exposures from 1/10,000 to 1 second. For a 10 second exposure add one stop. Not recommended for exposure beyond 10 seconds.

Grain: Moderate

Degree of enlargement: Moderately low

Resolving power: 80 lines/mm

Color rendition: Neutral colors

Exposure latitude: +2/–1 stop

Contrast: Medium

Processing: C-41 or equivalent

Push-processing: Not recommended

Format: 35mm

Uses: A high-speed, relatively fine-grain film for use in low light or when high shutter speeds/minimum apertures are required.

Comments: The wide exposure latitude of this film permits improved results when lighting conditions are difficult to meter. It can also be exposed under artificial light without filters and then printed with corrections for pleasing results. This is Kodak's premium film in the high-speed arena.

EKTAPRESS GOLD 1600

Manufacturer: Eastman Kodak

Designation: 5030, Professional

Speed: ISO 1600

Balanced for: Daylight/electronic flash

Reciprocity effect: No compensation required for exposures in 1/10,000 to 1 second range. Add 1 stop for a 10 second exposure. Not recommended for exposures longer than 10 seconds.

Grain: Moderate

Degree of enlargement: Moderately low

Resolving power: 80 lines/mm

Color rendition: Rich, neutral colors

Exposure latitude: +/−1 stop

Contrast: Medium

Processing: C-41 or equivalent

Push-processing: For EI 3200, add 30 seconds to developing time; for EI 6400, add 1 minute to developing time.

Format: 35mm

Uses: A fast color negative film for photo-journalism, sports and action photography, or in low light. Film can be pushed to higher ratings.

Comments: This pushable color negative film allows for great versatility in capturing extreme low-light action. Pushing yields higher grain and an increase in contrast, but it also brings new speed ratings to color negative shooters. An entire roll must be rated and developed to obtain the same speed. Kodak claims this film, although professional, doesn't need refrigeration to maintain balance and speed specifications.

FUJICOLOR SUPER HG 1600

Manufacturer: Fuji

Designation: Amateur

Speed: ISO 1600

Balanced for: Daylight/electronic flash

Reciprocity effect: In 1/10,000 to 1/10 sec. range, no compensation is required. For 1 second exposure, add 1/2 stop; for a 10 second exposure, add 1 1/2 stops; for a 100 second exposure, add 2 1/2 stops.

Grain: Moderate

Degree of enlargement: Moderately low

Resolving power: Not available

Color rendition: Rich colors

Exposure latitude: +2/−1 stop

Contrast: Medium to medium high

Processing: C-41 or equivalent

Push-processing: Not recommended

Format: 35mm

Uses: For low-light or action photography indoors. Can be used outdoors when fast shutter speeds and/or narrow apertures are required.

Comments: This updated fast color-print film from Fuji brings good grain for the speed and color richness to those needing the extra speed. Special spectral sensitivity allows for good color results even when the film is exposed under artificial illumination. It may provide too much contrast under bright lighting conditions outdoors, but overall it yields very pleasing results.

COLOR
NEGATIVE FILMS
ISO 1600

KODACOLOR GOLD 1600

Manufacturer: Eastman Kodak

Designation: Amateur

Speed: ISO 1600

Balanced for: Daylight/electronic flash

Reciprocity effect: No filtration or exposure compensation is required for shutter speeds from 1/10,000 to 1 second. For a 10 second exposure, add 1 stop. Not recommended for exposures longer than 10 seconds.

Grain: Moderate

Degree of enlargement: Moderately low

Resolving power: 80 lines/mm

Color rendition: Neutral, rich colors

Exposure latitude: +2/–1 stop

Contrast: Medium to medium high

Processing: C-41 or equivalent

Push-processing: Not recommended

Format: 35mm

Uses: Designed for low-light and fast action situations, this film is useful when shooting sports or special events indoors without flash. It can also be used for candid snapshots indoors.

Comments: This film replaces the previous Kodak high-speed amateur print film, VR-1000. It offers improved color saturation and reproduction. Because the film is often used indoors under artificial light conditions, Kodak has designed it to yield good color reproduction under tungsten illumination. In addition, this film offers good tonal gradation under low-light conditions.

KONICA SR-G 3200

Manufacturer: Konica

Designation: Amateur

Speed: ISO 3200

Balanced for: Daylight/electronic flash

Reciprocity effect: No filtration or exposure compensation required for exposures in 1/10,000 to 1 second range. For 10 second exposures, add 1/2 stop; for 100 second exposures, add 1 stop.

Grain: Moderate to coarse

Degree of enlargement: Low

Resolving power: Not available

Color rendition: Neutral

Exposure latitude: +/−$^1/_2$ to 1 stop

Contrast: Medium high

Processing: C-41

Push-processing: Not recommended

Format: 35mm, 120

Uses: For handheld photography in extremely low light; also for sports and action shooting when high shutter speeds are required indoors. Lack of color shifting during long exposures makes it suitable for astronomical photography.

Comments: This is the fastest color negative film ever made that, despite its fast speed, delivers a highly usable image. Fans of fine grain might object to the coarse grain, but they will be impressed with the results at this previously unheard-of rating. This film opens up photographic possibilities and image acquisition previously unavailable to photographers.

COLOR TRANSPARENCY FILMS

ISO25
Kodachrome 25 Professional, 25
Amateur

ISO40
Kodachrome 40 Type A
Professional

ISO50
Agfachrome 50 RS Professional
Ektachrome 50 HC
Ektachrome 50 Professional
Fujichrome 50
Fujichrome 50 Professional
Fujichrome Velvia

ISO64
Ektachrome 64 Professional
Ektachrome 64 Professional EPV
Ektachrome 64 Professional EPX
Ektachrome 64T Professional
Fujichrome 64T Professional
Kodachrome 64 Professional, 64
Amateur

ISO100
Agfachrome CT 100
Agfachrome 100 RS Professional
Ektachrome 100 HC
Ektachrome 100 Plus Professional
Ektachrome 100 Professional
Fujichrome 100
Fujichrome 100 Professional D
ScotchChrome 100

ISO160
Ektachrome 160 Professional,
160 Amateur

ISO200
Agfachrome CT 200
Agfachrome 200 RS Professional
Ektachrome 200 Professional,
200 Amateur
Kodachrome 200 Professional,
200 Amateur

ISO400
Ektachrome 400
Fujichrome 400
Fujichrome 400 Professional D
ScotchChrome 400

ISO640
ScotchChrome 640T

ISO1000
Agfachrome 1000 RS
Professional
ScotchChrome 1000

ISO1600
Ektachrome P800/1600
Professional
Fujichrome P1600 Professional D

Special Purpose
Ektachrome Duplicating Films
Vericolor Slide Film

Alternately known as color transparency, color slide, positive, chrome, or reversal film, the slide films in this category are used to make color slides for projection, for reproductions in magazines and books, and for prints and display materials. The films break down into two major categories—E-6 and Kodachrome films. The E-6 films have dye-producing color couplers incorporated in their emulsion, while Kodachrome films have color dyes added during the development process. The Kodachrome development process, K-14, is a long and involved affair; E-6 processing is done by far more laboratories around the world. However, when stored properly, Kodachrome-type films still offer the best stability of any type of photographic film available today. The stability of E-6 has improved substantially and, in fact, it is more stable than Kodachrome when slides are subjected to frequent projection.

Slide film is roughly divided into daylight- and tungsten-balanced types with the vast majority being daylight-balanced film. Tungsten films are used for copy work and studio photography—or any time tungsten light sources are used. If exposed in daylight, tungsten-balanced films have a blue cast. However, appropriate color-balancing filters can be used to adjust nearly any film to almost any light source.

Conventional transparency films are available in the ISO 25 to 1000 range. There are also special push-process films that allow photographers to use exposure indexes (EIs) of 3200 and beyond, albeit with diminishing quality (increases in grain and contrast) when the speed is increased. In the past, only E-6 films were pushed. Today, since more custom labs are handling Kodachrome, these films are being pushed as well. In fact, many photographers have expressed a preference for using Kodachrome 200 exposed and processed at EI 500, rather than at its suggested rating.

Slide films can be more finicky than color negative films—they tend to have more contrast and have considerably less exposure latitude. Despite their challenging nature, slide films still command the loyalty of millions of photographers worldwide. In addition, magazines, books, greeting cards, and so forth still use color slides as their source material for reproductions. The commercial and professional uses of color transparency film make it a major topic of interest to all professional and advanced amateur photographers.

FILM FOR COLOR SLIDES

Kodachrome

25

KM 135-36

36 EXP

35 mm

KODACHROME 25 PROFESSIONAL, 25 AMATEUR

Manufacturer: Eastman Kodak

Designation: PKM, Professional; KM, Amateur

Speed: ISO 25

Balanced for: Daylight/electronic flash

Reciprocity effect: For exposures in 1/10,000 to 1/10 sec. range no compensation is required. For a 1 second exposure, add 1/2 stop. Not recommended for exposures longer than 1 second.

Grain: Extremely fine

Degree of enlargement: Extremely high

Resolving power: 100 lines/mm

Color rendition: True, rich colors

Exposure latitude: +/–1 stop

Contrast: Medium

Processing: K-14

Format: 35mm

Push-processing: Not recommended

Uses: A slow-speed slide film for landscapes and general pictorial photography.

Comments: Long providing the standard of comparison for all other slide films, Kodachrome 25 affords the finest grain, best sharpness, and longest dark storage stability of any transparency film. Being a professional emulsion, PKM should be stored in refrigerated conditions prior to exposure and processed as soon as possible after exposure. Under appropriate lighting conditions, this is the film of choice for many photographers.

KODACHROME 40 TYPE A PROFESSIONAL

Kodachrome
40 Type A

36 EXPOSURES
KPA 135-36

Manufacturer: Eastman Kodak

Designation: KPA, Professional

Speed: ISO 40

Balanced for: 3400K photolamps

Reciprocity effect: No compensation is required for exposures in 1/10,000 to 1/10 sec. range. Add 1/2 stop for a 1 second exposure; add 1 stop for a 5 second exposure; not recommended for exposures at or beyond 10 seconds.

Grain: Extremely fine

Degree of enlargement: Very high

Resolving power: 100 lines/mm

Color rendition: Rich, neutral colors

Exposure latitude: +/–1 stop

Contrast: Medium

Processing: K-14

Push-processing: Not recommended

Format: 35mm

Uses: For color copy work, macro photography, and other work when using 3400K photolamps for illumination.

Comments: A unique copy film, Kodachrome 40 Type A is specifically balanced for 3400K photolamps. It is a very sharp, extremely fine-grain film. It can also be used for studio work where photolamps, such as those used in reflectors, are used for illumination. Some photographers mount an 85 filter on their lens and use this film in daylight as well.

AGFACHROME 50 RS PROFESSIONAL

Manufacturer: Agfa

Designation: Professional

Speed: ISO 50

Balanced for: Daylight/electronic flash

Reciprocity effect: No compensation is required for exposures in 1/10,000 to 1/100 sec. range. For a 1/10 sec. exposure, add a 025B filter; for a 1 second exposure, add 1/2 stop and a 050B filter; for a 10 second exposure, add 1 stop and a 075B filter.

Grain: Very fine

Degree of enlargement: High

Resolving power: Not available

Color rendition: Rich, saturated colors

Exposure latitude: +/−1 stop

Contrast: Medium

Processing: E-6 or equivalent

Push-processing: For a 1 stop push, add 2 to 3 minutes to first developing time.

Format: 35mm, 120, 4 × 5, 8 × 10

Uses: A fine-grain, sharp professional slide film for landscapes, portraits, and general professional photography.

Comments: In the past, Agfachrome Professional slide films were known for a neutral-to-warm color rendition with somewhat subdued contrast. The "European" color of these films was well known. Now Agfa has switched to a more color-saturated look in all their professional chrome films. Though somewhat slow in speed, the ISO 50 emulsion delivers very fine grain, excellent sharpness, and rich colors that make it useful for a wide range of photographic applications.

EKTACHROME 50 HC

Manufacturer: Eastman Kodak

Designation: HC, Amateur

Speed: ISO 50

Balanced for: Daylight/electronic flash

Reciprocity effect: No compensation required for exposures in 1/10,000 to 1/10 sec. range. For a 1 second exposure, add 1/2 stop and an 05R filter. Not recommended for exposures longer than 1 second.

Grain: Very fine

Degree of enlargement: High

Resolving power: Not available

Color rendition: Rich, saturated colors

Exposure latitude: +/–1 stop

Contrast: Medium

Processing: E-6 or equivalent

Push-processing: For a 1 stop push, add 2 to 3 minutes to first developer time.

Format: 35mm

Uses: This slow-speed color-slide film is used for general-purpose photography.

Comments: Designed for projection or prints, this slow-speed film offers rich color saturation, excellent sharpness, and fine grain. The HC code in the Kodak Ektachrome brand designates a highly color-saturated amateur slide film.

EKTACHROME 50 PROFESSIONAL

Manufacturer: Eastman Kodak

Designation: EPY, Professional

Speed: ISO 50

Balanced for: Tungsten 3200K

Reciprocity effect: Not recommended for exposures in 1/10,000 to 1/1000 sec. range; not recommended for exposures in 10 to 100 seconds and longer range. For a 1/100 sec. exposure, add an 05C filter. No compensation required for a 1/10 sec. exposure. For a 1 second exposure, add an 05R filter.

Grain: Very fine

Degree of enlargement: High

Resolving power: 125 lines/mm

Color rendition: Rich, neutral colors

Exposure latitude: +/–1 stop

Contrast: Medium

Processing: E-6 or equivalent

Push-processing: For a 1 stop push, add 2-3 minutes to first developer time.

Format: 35mm, 35mm long roll, 120

Uses: This professional transparency film is appropriate for studio and location work where tungsten illumination is used.

Comments: This studio standard for tungsten lighting setups has excellent grain and sharpness. Note that speed and color balance are tested for each batch of film, so check the instruction sheet packaged with the film for optimum results.

FUJICHROME 50

Manufacturer: Fuji

Designation: RF, Amateur

Speed: ISO 50

Balanced for: Daylight/electronic flash

Reciprocity effect: Within 1/10,000 to 1 second range, no adjustment in filtration or exposure is required. For a 4 second exposure, add 1/3 stop and a 5M filter; for a 16 second exposure, add 10M and 2/3 stop; for a 32 second exposure, add 12.5M filter and 1 stop.

Grain: Extremely fine

Degree of enlargement: High

Resolving power: 125 lines/mm

Color rendition: Very rich, saturated colors

Exposure latitiude: +/–1 stop

Contrast: Medium

Processing: E-6 or equivalent

Push-processing: +1 stop yields additional color contrast; add 2-3 minutes to first developer.

Format: 35mm

Uses: A fairly slow, but very sharp, fine-grain slide film for landscape and general photography. Optimal for projection, although color prints can also be made.

Comments: This amateur ISO 50 film exhibits extremely high color saturation. Fuji excels in high saturation films, and this film leads that line. Underexposure by 1/3 stop increases color richness, providing a "wet paint" look to blues and yellows, and adding richness to reds. The film's slow speed inhibits the use of a telephoto lens without a tripod, except on the brightest days. This improved emulsion purportedly decreases quality-control problems in processing.

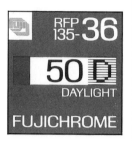

FUJICHROME 50 PROFESSIONAL

Manufacturer: Fuji

Designation: RFP, Professional

Speed: ISO 50

Balanced for: Daylight/electronic flash

Reciprocity effect: No filtration or exposure compensation is required for exposures in 1/10,000 to 1 second range. For exposures of 4 seconds, add 1/3 stop and a 5M filter; for 8 second exposures, add 1/2 stop and 7.5M filter; for 16 second exposures, add 2/3 stop and a 10M filter; for 32 second exposures, add 1 stop and a 12.5M filter. Not recommended for exposures of 64 seconds or longer.

Grain: Extremely fine

Degree of enlargement: High

Resolving power: 125 lines/mm

Color rendition: Rich, saturated colors

Exposure latitude: +1/−1 stop

Contrast: Medium to medium high

Processing: E-6 or equivalent

Push-processing: +1 stop add 2-3 minutes in first developer.

Format: 35mm, 120, 4 × 5, 8 × 10, 11 × 14

Uses: This film lends itself to photomechanical reproduction of commercial, fashion, industrial, stock, and art photography.

Comments: Though the film's speed is slow, color rendition, sharpness, and grain are excellent. The spectral absorption characteristics of the color dyes and gray balance of Fujichrome 50 Professional are tailored for scanner color separation, and it is therefore excellent for photomechanical reproduction. Colors are extremely vivid, and the film may add an edge of surreal color to landscapes and portraits.

FUJICHROME VELVIA

Manufacturer: Fuji

Designation: RVP, Professional

Speed: ISO 50

Balanced for: Daylight/electronic flash

Reciprocity effect: For exposures in 1/10,000 to 1 second range, no compensation is required. For 4 second exposures add 1/3 stop and a 5M filter; for 8 second exposures, add 1/2 stop and 7.5M filter; for 16 second exposures, add 2/3 stop and a 10M filter; for 32 second exposures, add 1 stop and a 12.5M filter. Exposures of 64 seconds and longer are not recommended.

Grain: Extremely fine

Degree of enlargement: High

Resolving power: 160 lines/mm

Color rendition: Rich, vibrant colors

Exposure latitude: +/−1 stop

Contrast: Medium

Processing: E-6 or equivalent

Push-processing: +1 stop, add 2-3 minutes in first developer.

Format: 35mm, 35 long roll, 120, 220, 4 × 5, 8 × 10, 11 × 14

Uses: A professional-quality slide film for landscapes, portraits, and commercial photography where bold color rendition is desired.

Comments: Fuji Velvia combines rich, vibrant colors with a very neutral contrast; the result is excellent color separation, especially when subtle distinction between colors is desired with excellent grain and sharpness. Velvia shows very good separation in shadow details, and maximum densities are very rich. Unlike some slide films that require slight underexposure for extra color richness, Velvia sacrifices neither image nor color richness under normal exposure.

Kodak

Ektachrome

64 Daylight
PROFESSIONAL FILM
8, 10, 12, OR 16 EXP

EPR 120

EKTACHROME 64 PROFESSIONAL

Manufacturer: Eastman Kodak

Designation: EPR; 6117 (sheet film); Professional

Speed: ISO 64

Balanced for: Daylight/electronic flash

Reciprocity effect: No compensation required in range of 1/10,000 to 1/10 sec. Add 1/2 stop and a 10M filter for 1 second exposure; add 1 1/2 stops and a 15M filter for a 10 second exposure. Not recomended for exposures beyond 10 seconds.

Grain: Very fine

Degree of enlargement: High

Resolving power: 125 lines/mm

Color rendition: Rich, neutral colors

Exposure latitude: +/−1 stop

Contrast: Medium

Processing: E-6 or equivalent

Push-processing: For 1 stop push, add 2 to 3 minutes to first developer time.

Format: 35mm, 35mm long roll, 46mm long roll, 70mm long roll, 120, 220, 4 × 5, 5 × 7, 8 × 10, 11 × 14

Uses: A transparency film for studio, location, portrait, industrial, and other professional uses.

Comments: This long-standing film has the loyalty of many professional photographers. It delivers highly consistent results with very fine grain, excellent sharpness, and true-to-life, natural colors. Considered a standard in many studios, it has yet to yield to the trend in high color saturation.

EKTACHROME 64 PROFESSIONAL EPV

Manufacturer: Eastman Kodak

Designation: EPV, Professional

Balanced for: Daylight/electronic flash

Reciprocity effect: No compensation required for exposures between 1/10,000 and 1/10 sec. Add 1/2 stop and 10M filter for 1 second exposures; add 1 1/2 stops and a 15M filter for 10 second exposures. Not recommended for exposures over 10 seconds.

At press time, manufacture of this film was discontinued.

Grain: Very fine

Degree of enlargement: High

Resolving power: 125 lines/mm

Color rendition: Rich, neutral colors

Exposure latitude: +/–1 stop

Contrast: Medium

Processing: E-6 or equivalent

Push-processing: For 1 stop, add 2 to 3 minutes to first developer time.

Format: 35mm

Uses: This general-purpose slide film is available in a 5 or 50 roll Press-Pac.

Comments: Designed for the large-volume user, this film has fine grain, good sharpness, and rich, neutral color rendition.

COLOR TRANSPARENCY FILMS

ISO 64

EKTACHROME 64 PROFESSIONAL EPX

Manufacturer: Eastman Kodak

Designation: EPX, Professional

Speed: ISO 64

Balanced for: Daylight/electronic flash

Reciprocity effect: No compensation is required for exposures in the 1/10,000 to 1/10 sec. range. For a 1 second exposure, add a CC05R filter and increase exposure by 1/2 stop. Not recommended for exposures longer than 1 second.

Grain: Very fine

Degree of enlargement: High

Resolving power: 125 lines/mm

Color rendition: Rich, neutral colors

Exposure latitude: +/–1 stop

Contrast: Medium

Processing: E-6 or equivalent

Push-processing: For a 1 stop push, add 2 to 3 minutes to first developer.

Format: 35mm, 120

Uses: This professional color transparency film is intended for outdoor use and when a warmer color balance than that provided by other Ektachrome films is desired.

Comments: This new addition to the Ektachrome line features added warmth (less blue), fine grain, excellent sharpness, and very good flesh-tone reproduction. Suited for outdoor photography, it delivers good results on sunlit and overcast days.

EKTACHROME 64T PROFESSIONAL

Manufacturer: Eastman Kodak

Designation: 5018, Professional

Speed: ISO 64

Balanced for: Tungsten illumination/3200K

Reciprocity effect: No compensation is required for exposures in a 1/100 to 10 second range. For a 100 second exposure, add 1/3 stop. See instructions packaged with film for speed and recommendations for particular emulsion batch.

Grain: Very fine

Degree of enlargement: High

Resolving power: 125 lines/mm

Color rendition: Rich, neutral colors

Exposure latitude: +/–1 stop

Contrast: Medium

Processing: E-6 or equivalent

Push-processing: Not recommended

Format: 35mm, 35mm and 70mm long roll, 120

Uses: This sheet film is intended for studio and interior architectural work under tungsten (3200K) illumination. Useful for photomechanical reproduction, direct duplication, and making prints.

Comments: The film offers improved reciprocity charactistics over the former Kodak Ektachrome Professional. Used widely for product photography under tungsten lighting conditions, its primary applications are for advertising illustrations and copying artwork.

COLOR TRANSPARENCY FILMS

ISO 64

FUJICHROME 64T PROFESSIONAL

Manufacturer: Fuji

Designation: RTP, Professional

Speed: ISO 64

Balanced for: Tungsten illumination/3100K

Reciprocity effect: No exposure compensation or filtration is required when exposures are made in the 1/4000 to 16 second range. For a 32 second exposure, add 1/3 stop; for a 64 second exposure, add 1/2 stop and a 2.5B filter.

Grain: Very fine

Degree of enlargement: High

Resolving power: 125 lines/mm

Color rendition: Rich, saturated colors

Exposure latitude: +/−^{1}/$_2$ to 1 stop

Contrast: Medium

Processing: E-6 or equivalent

Push-processing: For a 1 stop push, add 2-3 minutes to first developer.

Format: 35mm, 35mm long roll, 120, 4 × 5, 8 × 10

Uses: This film is meant for product, interior, architectural photography, as well as illustration and closeup work when tungsten illumination is used, and it has applications in scientific, medical, industrial research, and photomicrographic work as well.

Comments: This improved Fuji tungsten-balanced slide film yields highly saturated colors and has excellent extended exposure time capability. Neutral gray balance has been improved, as well as the film's ability to hold color and contrast even when push-processed. Excellent highlight-to-deep shadow reproduction makes it well suited for product photography where texture and color are important. Film pushed one stop shows virtually no color shift.

KODACHROME 64 PROFESSIONAL, 64 AMATEUR

Manufacturer: Eastman Kodak

Designation: PKR, Professional; KR, Amateur

Speed: ISO 64

Balanced for: Daylight/electronic flash

Reciprocity effect: Recommended exposure times are in 1/10,000 to 1/10 sec. range. For 1 second exposure, add 1 stop and a 10R filter. Not recommended for exposures longer than 1 second.

Grain: Extremely fine

Degree of enlargement: Very high

Resolving power: 100 lines/mm

Color rendition: Rich, neutral colors

Exposure latitude: +/–1 stop

Contrast: Medium

Processing: K-14

Push-processing: Film can be pushed by a professional lab, but it's usually not recommended.

Format: 35mm, 120, professional; 35mm, amateur

Uses: This general-purpose transparency film is appropriate for studio and location work, stock, fashion, and other professional uses. The amateur version is a standard for color-slide photography.

Comments: Over 1 stop faster than Kodachrome 25 Professional, PKR offers exceptionally fine grain, sharpness, and color rendition and is favored over PKM in the field because of its faster speed. Kodachrome films are also extremely stable and long-lasting when properly stored. The standard for color-slide shooters, PKR retains its popularity as the slide film to which all others are compared. The 120 size brings these qualities to medium-formats.

COLOR TRANSPARENCY FILMS

ISO 100

AGFA

For color slides

AGFACHROME

CT 100

135 36 EXCL.

AGFACHROME CT 100

Manufacturer: Agfa

Designation: Amateur

Speed: ISO 100

Balanced for: Daylight/electronic flash

Reciprocity effect: For exposures between 1/10 and 1/1000 sec. no compensation is required. For exposures longer than 1/10 sec., color will shift toward yellow; for exposures shorter than 1/1000 sec., color will shift toward blue. These deviations can be corrected by proper filtration; manufacturer suggests testing by trial exposures.

Grain: Fine

Degree of enlargement: Moderate

Resolving power: Not available

Color rendition: Rich, saturated colors

Exposure latitude: +/–1 stop

Contrast: Medium

Processing: E-6 or equivalent

Push-processing: Not recommended

Format: 35mm

Uses: A general-purpose amateur color-slide film.

Comments: Agfa's ISO 100 slide film offers rich, saturated colors, moderately fine grain, and a pleasing color rendition.

AGFACHROME 100 RS PROFESSIONAL

Manufacturer: Agfa

Designation: Professional

Speed: ISO 100

Balanced for: Daylight/electronic flash

Reciprocity effect: No compensation is required for exposures in 1/10,000 to 1/100 sec. range. For a 1/10 sec. exposure, add an 025B filter; for a 1 second exposure, add 1/2 stop and a 050B filter; for a 10 second exposure, add 1 stop and a 075B filter.

Grain: Very fine

Degree of enlargement: Moderately high

Resolving power: Not available

Color rendition: Rich, saturated color

Exposure latitude: +/–1 stop

Contrast: Medium

Processing: E-6 or equivalent

Push-processing: Add 2 to 3 minutes to first developer for a 1 stop push.

Format: 35mm, 120, 9 × 12cm, 4 × 5, 8 × 10

Uses: A medium-speed slide film for professional photography, including portraits, landscapes, and architectural work.

Comments: The Agfa professional slide films have seen a recent increase in overall color saturation. This ISO 100 film yields very rich colors, excellent sharpness, and fine grain. It is also more neutral, as opposed to warm in previous Agfa slide films, in overall color rendition.

COLOR
TRANSPARENCY FILMS
ISO 100

EKTACHROME 100 HC

Manufacturer: Eastman Kodak

Designation: HC, Amateur

Speed: ISO 100

Balanced for: Daylight/electronic flash

Reciprocity effect: No compensation required for exposures in 1/10,000 to 1/10 sec. range. For a 1 second exposure, add 1/2 stop and an CC05R filter. Not recommended for exposures longer than 1 second.

Grain: Fine

Degree of enlargement: Moderately high

Resolving power: 100 lines/mm

Color rendition: Rich, saturated colors

Exposure latitude: +/–1 stop

Contrast: Medium

Processing: E-6 or equivalent

Push-processing: For EI 200, add 2-3 minutes to first developer time.

Format: 35mm

Uses: A general-purpose amateur color slide film for projection or prints.

Comments: Though grain and sharpness are equivalent to Ektachrome 100 film, the HC code denotes a film with high color saturation. This film has fine grain, excellent sharpness, and is a good all-round choice for travel, family pictures, and other amateur uses where high color saturation is desired.

EKTACHROME 100 PLUS PROFESSIONAL

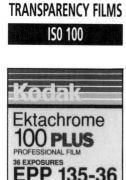

Manufacturer: Eastman Kodak

Designation: EPP, Professional; 5005 (35mm); 6005 (roll film); 6105 (sheet film); 5000 (EPW in Press-Pac).

Speed: ISO 100

Balanced for: Daylight/electronic flash

Color sensitivity: No adjustments or filters for exposures between 1/10,000 and 1/10 sec. Add a CC05R filter and 1 stop for 1 second exposure. Longer exposure times not recommended.

Grain: Fine grain

Degree of enlargement: High

Resolving power: 100 lines/mm

Color rendition: Rich, saturated colors

Exposure latitude: +/–1 stop

Contrast: Medium

Processing: E-6 or equivalent

Push-processing: One stop increase developing time 2-3 minutes; two stops increase developing time 4-6 minutes.

Format: 35mm, 120, 220, 4 × 5, 5 × 7, 8 × 10, 11 × 14; pre-loaded 4 × 5 Readyload Packets, Press-Pacs of 50 rolls of 35mm

Uses: A versatile slide film used for projection slides, prints from slides, and for photomechanical reproduction.

Comments: The Kodak version of a highly saturated professional color slide film. As an alternative to the more moderately saturated Ektachrome lineup, it offers very good neutral color and fleshtone reproduction as well as a very good grain for the speed, excellent sharpness, and good tonal range. As an alternative to Fujichrome 100, this film offers a slightly more cool-to-neutral color rendition.

EKTACHROME 100 PROFESSIONAL

Manufacturer: Eastman Kodak

Designation: EPN, Professional; 6122 (sheet film)

Speed: ISO 100

Balanced for: Daylight/electronic flash

Reciprocity effect: No filtration or exposure compensation is required when exposing in 1/10,000 to 1/10 sec. range. Not recommended for exposures longer than 1/10 sec. When using multiple pops with electronic flash, add 1/3 stop for 4 pops; 1/2 stop and a 05M filter for 8 pops; and 2/3 stop and a 05M filter for 16 pops. No compensation required for up to 4 pops.

Grain: Very fine

Degree of enlargement: High

Resolving power: 100 lines/mm

Color rendition: Neutral, rich colors

Exposure latitude: +/–1 stop

Contrast: Medium

Processing: E-6 or equivalent

Push-processing: For a 1 stop push, add 2-3 minutes in first developer; for a 2 stop push add 4-6 minutes in first developer.

Format: 35mm, 35mm long roll, 120, 220, 4 × 5, 5 × 7, 8 × 10, 11 × 14

Uses: A general-purpose professional transparency film for commercial photography.

Comments: This well-known Ektachrome flagship film is an alternative to the higher color saturation of Ektachrome 100 Plus. Its modified spectral dye sensitivity accommodates certain colors and fabrics (azo-dyed) that are usually difficult to reproduce. Its neutral, naturalistic colors are its main asset.

FUJICHROME 100

Manufacturer: Fuji

Designation: RD, Amateur

Speed: ISO 100

Balanced for: Daylight/electronic flash

Reciprocity effect: For exposures in 1/10,000 to 1 second range, no compensation is required. For a 4 second exposure, add 1/3 stop and a 5M filter; add 1/2 stop and a 7.5M filter for an 8 second exposure; for a 16 second exposure, add 2/3 stop and a 10M filter; for a 32 second exposure, add 1 stop and a 12.5M filter. Not recommended for exposures at or longer than 64 seconds.

Grain: Very fine

Degree of enlargement: High

Resolving power: 125 lines/mm

Color rendition: Very rich, saturated colors

Exposure latitude: +/–1 stop

Contrast: Medium to medium high

Processing: E-6 or equivalent

Push-processing: For 1 stop, add 2 to 3 minutes to first developer.

Format: 35mm

Uses: A general-purpose amateur slide film for projection or prints.

Comments: In many respects this film is a virtual clone of Fujichrome 100 Professional, except that, according to Fuji, it has been formulated more for projection and commercial prints than for photo-mechanical reproduction. It has vivid, highly saturated colors, good gradation between highlight and shadow, and can be used for a wide variety of picture-taking situations. This improved version also promises less variance in results from one emulsion batch to the next, and less change when subject to minor processing variations. Compared to Ektachrome, it offers a slightly warmer rendition.

FUJICHROME 100 PROFESSIONAL D

Manufacturer: Fuji

Designation: RDP, Professional

Speed: ISO 100

Balanced for: Daylight/electronic flash

Reciprocity effect: Exposures in 1/10,000 to 1 second range require no compensation. For a 4 second exposure, add 1/3 stop and a 5M filter; 8 second exposures require an additional 1/2 stop and a 7.5M filter; for 16 second exposures, add 2/3 stop and a 10M filter; for 32 second exposures, add 1 stop and a 12.5M filter. Not recommended for exposures at and longer than 64 seconds.

Grain: Very fine

Degree of enlargement: High

Resolving power: 125 lines/mm

Color rendition: Very rich, saturated colors

Exposure latitude: +/–1 stop

Contrast: Medium to medium high

Processing: E-6 or equivalent

Push-processing: For 1 stop push add 2-3 minutes in first developer.

Format: 35mm, 35mm long roll, 120, 220, 4 × 5, 8 × 10, 11 × 14, 9 × 12cm, 13 × 18cm

Uses: Designed for photomechanical reproduction of landscapes and stock photography, as well as exterior architecture, fashion, commercial, and other studio photography.

Comments: With slightly more grain and an additional stop in speed over its professional counterpart, Fujichrome 50 Professional, this film has become a favorite with professionals because of its one-stop faster speed. It offers very good grain and sharpness, with vivid, richly saturated colors that at times seem more vivid than reality.

SCOTCHCHROME 100

Manufacturer: 3M

Designation: Amateur

Speed: ISO 100

Balanced for: Daylight/electronic flash

Reciprocity effect: No compensation required for exposures in 1/10,000 to 1/10 sec. range. For a 1 second exposure, add 2/3 stop and an 05Y filter; for a 10 second exposure, add 1 1/2 stops and a 10R filter; for a 100 second exposure, add 2 1/2 stops and a 15R filter.

Grain: Fine

Degree of enlargement: Moderately high

Resolving power: 94 lines/mm

Color rendition: Rich, saturated colors

Exposure latitude: +/–1 stop

Contrast: Medium

Processing: E-6 or equivalent

Push-processing: For a 1 stop push, add 2-3 minutes to first developer time.

Format: 35mm

Uses: A general-purpose amateur slide film for projection and prints.

Comments: ScotchChrome 100 offers higher color saturation than Scotch slide films of the past, has better dye stability, and improved consistency when faced with processing variabilities. This film has a very pleasing tonal rendition and offers good stability when subjected to prolonged projection.

EKTACHROME 160 PROFESSIONAL, 160 AMATEUR

Manufacturer: Eastman Kodak

Designation: EPT, Professional; ET, Amateur

Speed: ISO 160

Balanced for: Tungsten illumination/3200K

Reciprocity effect: For 1/10,000 sec. exposure, add a 025G filter; for 1/1000 sec. exposure, add a 05C filter; no compensation required for exposures in 1/100 to 1/10 sec. range; add 1/2 stop and a 025M filter for a 1 second exposure. Exposures of 10 seconds or longer not recommended.

Grain: Fine

Degree of enlargement: Moderate

Resolving power: 100 lines/mm

Color rendition: Rich, neutral colors

Exposure latitude: +/−1 stop

Contrast: Medium

Processing: E-6 or equivalent

Push-processing: For EI 320, add 2 to 3 minutes to first developer time.

Format: 35mm, 35mm long roll (100 ft.), 120

Uses: A medium-fast tungsten-balanced slide film for location work, indoor sports and action, theater, and other interior work under tungsten lights.

Comments: Also known as high-speed tungsten Ektachrome, this film allows for handheld shooting in theaters, museums, and sports arenas where tungsten lighting is used and flash is prohibited. It provides good color under these conditions without using filters. When necessary, it can be pushed 1 stop with some increase in contrast and grain; a 2 stop push results in loss of image quality.

AGFACHROME CT 200

Manufacturer: Agfa

Designation: Amateur

Speed: ISO 200

Balanced for: Daylight/electronic flash

Reciprocity effect: No compensation is required for exposures in 1/10 to 1/1000 sec. range. Exposures longer than 1/10 sec. will result in a yellow color deviation; exposures shorter than 1/1000 sec. can cause a shift toward blue. Manufacturer recommends trial exposures with balancing filters for best color balance.

Grain: Moderately fine

Degree of enlargement: Moderate

Resolving Power: Not available

Color rendition: Rich, saturated colors

Exposure latitude: +/–1 stop

Contrast: Medium to medium high

Processing: E-6 or equivalent

Push-processing: Not recommended

Format: 35mm

Uses: A general-purpose medium-fast color-slide film for projection as well as prints.

Comments: Agfa's medium-fast amateur slide film offers medium-to-high color saturation and moderately fine grain.

COLOR TRANSPARENCY FILMS

ISO 200

AGFACHROME 200 RS PROFESSIONAL

Manufacturer: Agfa

Designation: Professional

Speed: ISO 200

Balanced for: Daylight/electronic flash

Reciprocity effect: For exposures in 1/10,000 to 1/10 sec. range, no exposure compensation is required. For a 1 second exposure, add 1/2 stop and a 025B filter; for a 10 second exposure, add 1 stop and a 050B filter.

Grain: Moderately fine

Degree of enlargement: Moderate

Resolving power: Not available

Color rendition: Rich, saturated colors

Exposure latitude: +/–1 stop

Contrast: Medium to medium high

Processing: E-6 or equivalent

Push-processing: Add 2 to 3 minutes to the first developer for a 1 stop push.

Format: 35mm, 120

Uses: A medium-fast professional slide film for action scenes when a higher shutter speed is required, or for moderately low-light photography.

Comments: Agfachrome 200 displays moderate grain with excellent sharpness. Its tonality and overall balance are quite pleasing. This is among the newer generation of Agfa professional chrome films that offer rich, saturated colors.

EKTACHROME 200 PROFESSIONAL, 200 AMATEUR

Manufacturer: Eastman Kodak

Designation: EPD, Professional; ED, Amateur

Speed: ISO 200

Balanced for: Daylight/electronic flash

Reciprocity effect: No compensation is required for exposures in 1/10,000 to 1/10 sec. range. For a 1 second exposure, add 1/2 stop. Not recommended for exposures in 10 to 100 second and longer range.

Grain: Fine

Degree of enlargement: Moderate

Resolving power: 125 lines/mm

Color rendition: Rich, neutral colors

Exposure latitude: +/–1 stop

Contrast: Medium

Processing: E-6 or equivalent

Push-processing: For 1 stop push, add 2 to 3 minutes to first developer time.

Format: 35mm, 120, 220

Uses: A medium-speed transparency film for moderately low-light or fast action photography.

Comments: Ektachrome 200 offers good image quality and bridges the speed gap when a film faster than ISO 100 is required. It can be used for handheld telephoto shots of outdoor sports and action photography or when greater depth of field is required. The film pushes well to EI 400.

COLOR TRANSPARENCY FILMS

ISO 200

FILM FOR COLOR SLIDES

Kodachrome

200

KL 135-24

24 EXP   35 mm

KODACHROME 200 PROFESSIONAL, 200 AMATEUR

Manufacturer: Eastman Kodak

Designation: PKL, Professional; KL, Amateur

Speed: ISO 200

Balanced for: Daylight/electronic flash

Reciprocity effect: Recommended exposures are in 1/10,000 to 1/10 sec. range. Not recommended for exposures longer than 1/10 sec.

Grain: Fine

Degree of enlargement: Moderate

Resolving power: 100 lines/mm

Color rendition: Rich colors

Exposure latitude: +/–1 stop

Contrast: Medium

Processing: K-14

Push-processing: Done only by professional Kodachrome lab; some photographers prefer this film exposed and processed for EI 500, a +1 1/2 stop push.

Format: 35mm

Uses: Very good for use with handheld telephoto lenses and in moderately low-light street shooting and travel photography situations.

Comments: This medium-fast speed member of the Kodachrome family is a welcome addition to those who want the benefit of Kodachrome longevity and quality for candid travel and street shooting. It has a slightly warm image tone and good grain for the speed. Many photographers push it to EI 500 with successful results.

EKTACHROME 400

Manufacturer: Eastman Kodak

Designation: EL, Amateur

Speed: ISO 400

Balanced for: Daylight/electronic flash

Reciprocity effect: No compensation required for exposures in 1/10,000 to 1/10 sec. range. Add 1/2 stop for a 1 second exposure; add 1 1/2 stops and a 10C filter for a 10 second exposure; add 2 1/2 stops and a 10C filter for a 100 second exposure.

Grain: Moderately fine for the speed

Degree of enlargement: Moderately low

Resolving power: 80 lines/mm

Color rendition: Neutral colors

Exposure latitude: +/–1 stop

Contrast: Medium to medium high

Format: 35mm, 120

Processing: E-6

Push-processing: Add 2 to 3 minutes to developing time for a 1 stop push.

Uses: A fast slide film for low light or when high shutter speeds are required.

Comments: This high-speed slide film has been a stable member of the Ektachrome family for years. Colors are neutral. This film is best used in low light, and can be pushed one stop with good results.

FUJICHROME 400

Manufacturer: Fuji

Designation: RH, Amateur

Speed: ISO 400

Balanced for: Daylight/electronic flash

Reciprocity effect: No compensation is required when exposed in 1/10,000 to 1 second range. For a 4 second exposure, add 1/3 stop and a 2.5Y filter; add 1/2 stop and a 2.5Y filter for a 16 second exposure; for a 64 second exposure, add 2/3 stop and a 5Y filter.

Grain: Moderate

Degree of enlargement: Moderate

Resolving power: 125 lines/mm

Color rendition: Rich colors

Exposure latitude: +/−1 stop

Contrast: Medium to medium high

Processing: E-6 or equivalent

Push-Processing: For EI 800, add 2 to 3 minutes to first developer; for EI 1600, add 4 to 6 minutes to first developer.

Format: 35mm

Uses: A moderately fast color-slide film intended for prints and projection. In daylight it is useful for freezing fast action, and very useful for low-light scenes.

Comments: For tungsten illumination, use an 80A filter; however, this decreases the film's effective speed to EI 100. Though it can be pushed, it may be preferable to choose a slide film specially formulated to handle push-processing. This sharp, fast film exhibits fairly fine grain for the speed. Contrast may be excessive in broad daylight.

FUJICHROME 400 PROFESSIONAL D

Manufacturer: Fuji

Designation: RHP, Professional

Speed: ISO 400

Balanced for: Daylight/electronic flash

Reciprocity effect: For exposures in 1/10,000 to 1 second range, no compensation is required. For a 4 second exposure, add 1/3 stop and a 2.5Y filter; for 16 second exposures, add 1/2 stop and a 2.5Y filter; for a 64 second exposure, add 2/3 stop and a 5Y filter.

Grain: Medium

Degree of enlargement: Moderate

Resolving power: 125 lines/mm

Color rendition: Rich, saturated colors

Exposure latitude: +/−1 stop

Contrast: Medium to medium high

Processing: E-6 or equivalent

Push-processing: For EI 800 add 2-3 minutes to first developer time.

Format: 35mm

Uses: A high-speed color slide film for use when high shutter speed or increased depth of field is required or when photographing in low light. Also for available light, although the film isn't balanced for tungsten lighting.

Comments: Being a professional Fujichrome, this film is specially made for photomechanical reproduction. It features rich colors and moderate contrast, though use in bright daylight may result in images with too much contrast. If you want to push, note that a "pushing" slide film may be better.

COLOR TRANSPARENCY FILMS

ISO 400

24 EXP 400

ScotchChrome™

35 mm DX

Film for Color Slides

SCOTCHCHROME 400

Manufacturer: 3M

Designation: Amateur

Speed: ISO 400

Balanced for: Daylight/electronic flash

Reciprocity effect: At ISO 400 no compensation is required for exposures in 1/10,000 to 1 second range. For 10 second exposure, add 1 stop and a 05Y filter; for 100 second exposure, add 2 stops and a 10Y filter. For EI 800 no compensation is required in the 1/10,000 to 10 second range; add a 05Y filter for 100 second exposures. No compensation is required in all speeds at EI 1600 and EI 3200.

Grain: Medium to high, depending upon EI

Degree of enlargement: Moderately low

Resolving power: 89 lines/mm

Color rendition: Rich, saturated colors

Exposure latitude: +/–1 stop

Contrast: Medium to medium high, depending upon EI

Processing: E-6 or equivalent

Push-processing: Add 3 minutes to first developer time for EI 800; 6 minutes for EI 1600; 9 minutes for EI 3200.

Format: 35mm

Uses: A general-purpose, fast, color slide film for low-light, fast shutter speeds, or minimal apertures.

Comments: This is perhaps the most color-saturated ISO 400 amateur color slide film available today. A good choice when the light is low and color richness is desired, pushing it 1 stop does not change the film's contrast, grain, or color significantly. A 2 stop push shows slight increase in grain, less sharpness, and some loss of color richness. The results of a 3 stop push are not gratifying. (Note: This film may be packaged as ScotchChrome 800/1600 P.)

SCOTCHCHROME 640T

Manufacturer: 3M

Designation: Amateur

Speed: ISO 640

Balanced for: Tungsten illumination/3200K

Reciprocity effect: No compensation is required for exposures in 1/10,000 to 1/10 sec. range. For a 1 second exposure add 1/2 stop; add 1 stop for a 10 second exposure; for a 100 second exposure add 2 stops and a 10Y filter.

Grain: High

Degree of enlargement: Low

Resolving power: 85 lines/mm

Color rendition: Neutral colors

Exposure latitude: +/–$^{1}/_{2}$ stop

Contrast: Medium

Processing: E-6 or equivalent

Push-processing: For EI 1250, add 2 to 3 minutes to the first developer time.

Uses: A fast tungsten-balanced slide film for handheld shooting with telephoto lenses in low light, or for flash-free photography of sports, action, and theater indoors when areas are illuminated with tungsten lighting.

Comments: This is the fastest tungsten-balanced slide film available. Though its degree of enlargement is low, its grain structure is such that big enlargements lend an impressionistic feel to images. Despite the fact that it is balanced for tungsten lighting, 3200K will yield good results even when color temperature of light source ranges from 2850K to 3400K.

AGFACHROME 1000 RS PROFESSIONAL

Manufacturer: Agfa

Designation: Professional

Speed: ISO 1000

Reciprocity effect: No compensation is required for exposures in 1/10,000 to 1/10 sec. range. Add 1/3 stop for a 1 second exposure; add 2/3 stop for a 10 second exposure.

Grain: Coarse

Degree of enlargement: Low

Resolving power: Not available

Color rendition: Neutral colors

Exposure latitude: +/–$^1/_2$ to 1 stop

Contrast: Medium

Processing: E-6 or equivalent

Push-processing: Add 3 minutes to first developer for a 1 stop push

Format: 35mm, 120

Uses: A fast professional slide film for extremely low lighting conditions.

Comments: This very fast film attains its speed without the need for push-processing; a 1 stop push yields EI 2000 without any appreciable loss in overall quality. Though actual use of such a film may be limited, there are special times when this fast speed can come in handy, such in as extreme low-light shooting, special-effects portraits, and still-life photography.

SCOTCHCHROME 1000

Manufacturer: 3M

Designation: Amateur

Speed: ISO 1000

Balanced for: Daylight/electronic flash

Reciprocity effect: No compensation is required for exposures in 1/10,000 to 1 second range. For a 10 second exposure, add 2/3 stop and a 10B filter; for a 100 second exposure, add 1 1/2 stops and a 15M filter.

Grain: Coarse

Degree of enlargement: Low

Resolving power: 67 lines/mm

Color rendition: Neutral colors

Exposure latitude: $+/-\frac{1}{2}$ stop

Contrast: Medium

Processing: E-6 or equivalent

Push-processing: For EI 2000, add 3 minutes to first developer time.

Format: 35mm

Uses: A very fast slide film for low light and when fast shutter speeds and narrow apertures are required.

Comments: Though possibly the grainiest conventional slide film available, a legion of photographers continually lobby Scotch to keep it the way it is. The ScotchChrome 1000 grain is unique, producing a truly impressionistic image when enlarged. The coarse grain structure has a beauty all its own. However, the fast speed means exposure is critical, and moderate underexposure can result in real loss of color quality.

COLOR TRANSPARENCY FILMS

ISO 1600

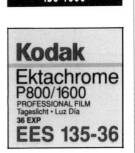

Kodak
Ektachrome
P800/1600
PROFESSIONAL FILM
Tageslicht • Luz Día
36 EXP
EES 135-36

EKTACHROME P800/1600 PROFESSIONAL

Manufacturer: Eastman Kodak

Designation: EES, Professional

Speed: Nominal speed is ISO 400. Made for pushing to EI 800, 1600, 3200.

Balanced for: Daylight/electronic flash

Reciprocity effect: For proper color rendition, use a CC10Y over lens when film is exposed at ISO 400. Made for exposures in range of 1/10,000 to 1/10 sec. Not recommended for exposures of 1 second or longer.

Grain: Medium at ISO 400; coarser as pushed speed increases

Degree of enlargement: Moderately low

Resolving power: At ISO 400 and EI 800, 80 lines/mm; at EI 1600 and 3200, 63 lines/mm

Color rendition: Neutral, tends toward blue

Exposure latitude: +/−$\frac{1}{2}$ to 1 stop

Contrast: Medium—tends toward medium-high when pushed

Processing: E-6 or equivalent

Push-processing: In first developer, add 2 to 3 minutes for 1 stop push; 4 to 7 minutes for 2 stop push; 6 to 9 minutes for 3 stop push.

Format: 35mm

Uses: A high-speed slide film designed for push-processing. It is best used for low-light photography.

Comments: Ektachrome P800/1600 comes in handy when lighting conditions can't be predicted beforehand and low light is the prevailing condition. Grain and contrast increase and sharpness decreases as speed is boosted.

FUJICHROME P1600 PROFESSIONAL D

Manufacturer: Fuji

Designation: RSP II, Professional

Speed: Nominal speed is ISO 400. Made for pushing to EI 800, 1600, 3200.

Balanced for: Daylight/electronic flash

Reciprocity effect: In 1/10,000 to 1 second range, no exposure compensation is required. Exposures of 4 seconds require additional 1/2 stop and a 2.5G filter; for 16 second exposures, add 1 stop and a 5G filter; for 64 second exposures, add 1 2/3 stop and a 5G filter.

Grain: Moderately fine at ISO 400; increases proportionately at EI 800, 1600, and 3200

Degree of enlargement: Moderate at ISO 400, moderately low at push speeds

Resolving power: Not available

Color rendition: Rich, neutral colors

Exposure latitude: +/−1 stop at ISO 400; slightly less at higher speeds

Contrast: Medium; higher as EI is raised

Processing: E-6 or equivalent

Push-processing: For EI 800, add 2 to 3 minutes to first developer time; for EI 1600, add 6 minutes; for EI 3200, add 9 minutes; for EI 4800, add 10 minutes.

Format: 35mm

Uses: An ISO 400 film made to be pushed. For indoor sports, theater, night photography, and astronomical photography.

Comments: This improved version of high-speed pushable slide film yields more natural colors and fuller tonal gradation than Fuji's original film at this speed.

Kodak
Ektachrome
SE Duplicating Film
SO-366
36 EXPOSURES
135-36

EKTACHROME DUPLICATING FILMS

Manufacturer: Eastman Kodak

Designation: 5071 (35mm, 35mm long rolls, 46mm long rolls); SO-366 (35mm, 35mm long rolls); 6121 (sheet films 4 × 5 through 16 × 20); 8071 (rolls); 7121 (sheets)

Speed: Varies—check film package. Generally ISO 12 to ISO 20

Balanced for: All are tungsten-balanced, except for SO-366, which is balanced for electronic flash.

Reciprocity effect: Expose within recommended times.

Grain: Fine

Degree of enlargement: Moderately high

Resolving power: 125 lines/mm

Color rendition: Rich, neutral colors

Exposure latitude: Test, expose within recommended times.

Contrast: Medium

Processing: E-6 or equivalent

Push-processing: Not recommended

Format: See designations above.

Uses: For making duplicate transparencies.

Comments: Although these films have been grouped together in this listing, each has a very distinct application and exposure recommendation. Also, various filter packs may have to be used when making duplicates from different emulsions. Check the packaged instruction sheets for details. Duplicates can be made with 5071 using a 35mm SLR and appropriate duplicating equipment, or with SO-366 with electronic flash and filters. The newest film to join this group is Type K, designed for duplicating Kodachrome slides. The code numbers are 8071 for roll film and 7121 for sheet film.

VERICOLOR SLIDE FILM

Manufacturer: Eastman Kodak

Designation: 5072 (100 ft. rolls, 35mm); SO-279 (35mm rolls)

Speed: See exposure data packed with film.

Balanced for: Tungsten illumination/3200K

Reciprocity effect: Expose within recommended times.

Grain: Fine

Degree of enlargement: High

Resolving power: 200 lines/mm

Color rendition: Rich, neutral colors

Contrast: Medium

Exposure latitude: Intended for exposure times of 1/4 to 8 seconds. Follow instructions packed with film.

Processing: C-41 or equivalent

Push-processing: Not recommended

Format: 35mm, 35mm long rolls

Uses: For producing positive transparencies from color negatives and internegatives by direct printing, this film can also be used to make reverse text slides.

Comments: This versatile film, intended for lab use, can also be used with copying and duplicating equipment that allows for filter-pack adjustment. As a starting point, use the following filter packs to print slides from these films: Vericolor II Professional, 20M+35Y; Kodacolor films, 20M+30Y; Vericolor HC Professional, 20M+30Y. Test as needed with other films. These filter packs are based on average emulsions of Vericolor slide film; check the individual packs for instructions. This filtration is for negatives exposed with daylight or electronic flash; if exposing with tungsten light, additional yellow filtration is required.

**Kodak
Vericolor
slide film
SO-279**

36 EXPOSURES

135-36

BLACK-AND-WHITE FILMS

ISO 25
Agfaortho 25 Professional
Agfapan APX 25 Professional
Technical Pan

ISO 50
Ilford Pan F

ISO 100
Agfapan APX 100 Professional
Ektapan
T-Max 100

ISO 125
Ilford FP4 Plus
Plus-X Pan Professional, Plus-X
  Pan
Verichrome Pan

ISO 200
Super-XX Pan Professional

ISO 400
Agfapan 400 Professional
Delta 400
Ilford HP5 Plus
Ilford XP2 400
Neopan 400 Professional
T-Max 400 Professional
Tri-X Pan, Tri-X Pan Professional

ISO 1000
Recording Film

ISO 1600
Neopan 1600

ISO 3200
T-Max P3200 Professional

Special Purpose
Professional Copy Film
High-Speed Infrared

Black-and-white films are used for a wide range of photographic activities, from journalism to copying to pictorial work. Though a long-term decline in use was noted during the seventies and eighties, a virtual rebirth of the medium has occurred in both volume of rolls sold and the interest of a new generation of photographers in black and white. However, for many amateur and professional photographers the love of black and white never went away.

Unlike color film where color dyes are created with the silver image and then the silver is removed, black and white is essentially a silver-based image. The end product of most black-and-white work is prints, although black-and-white transparencies can also be made.

An important aspect of black-and-white photography is the ability to change the results of exposure on film according to the way it is processed. Contrast, speed, and tonal rendition can be manipulated with various film developers, processing times, and temperatures. When prints are made, these tonal and contrast changes can be enhanced even further. A black-and-white negative and print lends itself to literally hundreds of interpretations and variations.

As with all films, the slower black-and-white films yield the finest grain and best sharpness. However, thanks to breakthroughs in crystal-growth technology, even those in the ISO 400 group yield excellent results and may be better suited to difficult lighting conditions encountered in the field. Black-and-white films also have greater exposure latitude than both color negative and transparency films (plus black-and-white films can withstand greater adjustments in development).

Aside from using development to change tonal and contrast renditions, many black-and-white films can be easily push-processed to raise their effective speed. Though extremes in pushing yield excessive grain and contrast, very fast black-and-white films allow for exposures up to and beyond EI 3200.

In addition to conventional films, some black-and-white films can be used for copy work or for creating high-contrast negatives. Although sometimes used in the field for special effects, special-purpose films are best suited for their intended purpose. Without a doubt, black and white has made a comeback, and all photographers are exploring new ways of utilizing its special charm.

AGFAORTHO 25 PROFESSIONAL

Manufacturer: Agfa

Designation: Professional

Speed: ISO 25 (Note: Though a speed rating is usually not given for document films such as Agfaortho 25, use ISO 25 as an exposure guide.)

Color sensitivity: Orthochromatic

Reciprocity effect: No compensation required for exposures in 1/10,000 to 1 second range. Add 2/3 stop for a 10 second exposure; add 1 1/3 stops for a 100 second exposure.

Grain: Extremely fine

Degree of enlargement: Very high

Resolving power: 350 lines/mm

Exposure latitude: Narrow

Contrast: High

Processing: For negatives, Refinal, 10 minutes; Rodinal 1:10, 4 minutes. For positives, use a standard reversal processing kit.

Push-processing: Not recommended

Format: 35mm, 120

Uses: Can be used as either a negative or positive film for producing transparencies from text and line originals.

Comments: This copy film has very high contrast and is useful for making copies of line drawings, graphs, and artwork. It can be used in the camera as well as in the lab, and it can be developed under red safelight conditions.

AGFAPAN APX 25 PROFESSIONAL

Manufacturer: Agfa

Designation: Professional

Speed: ISO 25

Color sensitivity: Panchromatic

Reciprocity effect: For exposures between 1/10,000 and 1/2 sec. no compensation is required. Add 1 stop for a 1 second exposure; add 1 1/2 stops for a 10 second exposure; add 2 stops for a 100 second exposure.

Grain: Extremely fine

Degree of enlargement: Very high

Resolving power: 200 lines/mm

Exposure latitude: +/−2 1/2 stops

Contrast: Medium

Processing: In Agfa-recommended developers at 68 degrees F: Refinal, 6 minutes; Rodinal 1:50, 10 minutes.

Push-processing: Not recommended

Format: 35mm, 120

Uses: For applications when sharpness and fine grain are important, or for big enlargements.

Comments: This extremely sharp film from Agfa has the potential to deliver negatives with a beautiful, rich tonal scale and extremely fine grain. The slow speed precludes the film's use in low light or with telephoto lenses without a tripod, but the results obtained deserve the extra effort. Some lab workers report results are particularly good with the Refinal developer.

Kodak
technical
pan film
ESTAR-AH Base

36 EXPOSURES

TP 135-36

TECHNICAL PAN

Manufacturer: Eastman Kodak

Designation: 2415 (35mm and 35mm long rolls); 4415 (sheet film); 6515 (120).

Speed: EI 25 to 320, depending on developer; ISO 25 for pictorial photography

Color sensitivity: Panchromatic, with extended red sensitivity

Reciprocity effect: See instructional sheet for ISO adjustments at various exposure times.

Grain: Extremely fine or ultra fine, depending on developer used

Degree of enlargement: Extremely high

Resolving power: With HC-110 developer, 320 lines/mm; with Kodak Technidol LC and Technidol Liquid developer, 400 lines/mm

Exposure latitude: Narrow

Contrast: Depending on developer: Kodalith, extremely high; HC-110, dilution B, high; D-76, moderate; Technidol LC or Liquid, low

Processing: For continuous tone, develop 35mm film in either Technidol LC or Technidol Liquid. Develop 120 film in Technidol Liquid only. For positives of high-contrast line art, use the Kodak T-Max 100 Direct Positive Film Developing outfit. Check package instructions for more information.

Push-processing: Not recommended.

Format: 35mm, 35mm long rolls, 120, 4 × 5, 8 × 10

Uses: For pictorial photography with extremely fine grain and sharpness, and high-contrast graphic arts applications.

Comments: An extremely versatile film, it can be used for up to 50X enlargements and developed in a wide range of developers. The one thing that holds true thoughout all applications is its very fine grain and excellent sharpness.

ILFORD PAN F

Manufacturer: Ilford

Designation: Amateur/Professional

Speed: ISO 50

Color sensitivity: Panchromatic

Reciprocity effect: No compensation required for exposures in 1/10,000 to 1/2 sec. range. For a 1 second exposure, add 1/2 stop; for a 10 second exposure add 1/2 stop.

Gain: Very fine

Degree of enlargement: High

Resolving power: Not available

Exposure latitude: +/–2 stops

Contrast: Medium

Processing: D-76, 6 minutes; Ilford Universal (1:9), 4 minutes

Push-processing: (This film is not intended for push-processing, but when using the following developers rate the film at indicated speeds.) When using Microphen, develop film for 4 1/2 minutes and rate at EI 64. When using Ilford Perceptol, develop film for 11 minutes and rate film at EI 25.

Format: 35mm, 120

Uses: A very fine-grain film for general shooting when big enlargements are required.

Comments: This standard low-speed black-and-white film offers excellent sharpness, a very smooth tonal range, and very fine grain. It produces rich, lustrous negatives that can translate the same results to prints.

AGFAPAN APX 100 PROFESSIONAL

Manufacturer: Agfa

Designation: Professional

Speed: ISO 100

Color sensitivity: Panchromatic

Reciprocity effect: No compensation is required in 1/10,000 to 1/2 sec. exposure range. Add 1 stop and reduce developing time 10% for 1 second exposure; add 2 stops and reduce developing time by 25% for 10 second exposure; add 3 stops and reduce developing time by 35% for 100 second exposure.

Grain: Very fine

Degree of enlargement: High

Resolving power: 150 lines/mm

Exposure latitude: +/−2 1/2 stops

Contrast: Medium

Processing: In Agfa-recommended developers at 68 degrees: Refinal, 6 minutes; Rodinal 1:50, 14 minutes.

Push-processing: Not recommended

Format: 35mm, 120, 35mm × 100 ft., 6 × 9cm, 9 × 12cm, 8 × 10

Uses: A medium-speed film for portraiture, landscapes, industrial, and general professional as well as advanced amateur photography.

Comments: This fine-grain, sharp film is for professionals, but advanced amateurs and art photographers have taken a liking to it as well. It delivers a very pleasing gradation of tone.

EKTAPAN

Manufacturer: Eastman Kodak

Designation: 4162, Professional

Speed: ISO 100

Color sensitivity: Panchromatic

Reciprocity effect: No compensation required in 1/10,000 to 1/10 sec. range. Add 1 stop and decrease developing time by 10% for a 1 second exposure; add 2 stops and decrease developing time by 20% for a 10 second exposure.

Grain: Fine

Degree of enlargement: High

Resolving power: 125 lines/mm

Exposure latitude: +/–2 stops

Contrast: Medium

Processing: At 68 degrees F: D-76, 8 minutes; HC-110 (dilution B), 4 1/2 minutes; Microdol X, 10 minutes.

Push-processing: Not recommended

Format: 70mm long rolls, 4 × 5, 5 × 7, 8 × 10, 9 × 12cm

Uses: Recommended for portraits and close-up work with electronic flash, although it can be used with all types of lighting.

Comments: This fine-grain film offers very good exposure latitude and excellent tonal gradation. It has a retouching layer on both sides of the film emulsion. Also, it is speed-matched to Kodak Ektachrome 100 Professional film, so both a color transparency and a black-and-white negative can be produced with the same exposure.

BLACK-AND-WHITE FILMS
ISO 100

T-MAX 100

Manufacturer: Eastman Kodak

Designation: 5052 (35mm); 6052 (120); 4052 (sheet film); Professional

Speed: ISO 100

Color sensitivity: Panchromatic, with less blue sensitivity than conventional films.

Reciprocity effect: For a 1/10,000 sec. exposure, add 1/3 stop. No compensation required in 1/1000 to 1/10 sec. range. For a 1 second exposure, add 1/3 stop; for a 10 second exposure, add 1/2 stop; for a 100 second exposure, add 1 stop.

Grain: Very fine

Degree of enlargement: Very high

Resolving power: 200 lines/mm

Exposure latitude: +3/−2 stops

Contrast: Medium/medium high

Processing: T-Max developer at 75 degrees F, 6 1/2 minutes; D-76 at 68 degrees F, 9 minutes; HC-110 (dilution B) at 68 degrees F, 7 minutes. For sheet film: tray processing, D-76 at 68 degrees F, 9 1/2 minutes.

Push-processing: At EI 200 no compensation in processing is required. Develop normally. For EI 800: T-Max developer at 75 degrees F, 9 minutes; D-76 at 68 degrees F, 11 minutes. For EI 800: T-Max developer at 75 degrees F, 10 1/2 minutes.

Format: 35mm, 120, 220, 4 × 5, 8 × 10

Uses: A professional film with exceptionally fine grain and excellent sharpness. Always useful when great enlargement is required.

Comments: Although it is often difficult to locate this film's very fine grain for focusing, it produces very sharp images even when big enlargements are made. It can also be used to copy black-and-white photos and for photomicrography, as well as an internegative and interpositive film.

ILFORD FP4 PLUS

Manufacturer: Ilford

Designation: FP4 Plus, Professional/Amateur

Speed: ISO 125

Color sensitivity: Panchromatic

Reciprocity effect: No compensation for exposures from 1/10,000 and 1/2 sec. For longer times, add approximately 1 stop. Testing recommended for exposures longer than 12 seconds.

Grain: Very fine

Degree of enlargement: Very high

Resolving power: Not available

Exposure latitude: +/–2 1/2 stops. Ilford claims printable negatives can be obtained even when film is overexposed by 5 stops.

Contrast: Medium

Processing: For ISO 125: Ilford Universal, 1:14, 6 minutes; ID-11 Plus, 1:1, 8 minutes; Kodak D-76, 1:1, 8 1/2 minutes.

Push-processing: For best quality, expose at rated speed. For EI 400, Microphen stock solution, 11 minutes; for EI 800, 16 minutes; for EI 1600, 16 minutes.

Format: 35mm, 120, 4 × 5

Uses: A very fine-grain, medium-contrast film for general photographic purposes.

Comments: FP4 Plus is a revision of FP4, a favorite of photographers for many years. The new film is highly versatile, with a smooth tonal gradation and scale, and offers finer grain than its predecessor. It has a very wide exposure latitude and can deliver printable results with gross overexposure and moderate underexposure. It sports a high-acutance emulsion that, when combined with fine-grain development, yields excellent quality with great enlargement. Fine-tuning its exposure and processing times allows customization with many developers.

BLACK-AND-WHITE FILMS

ISO 125

PLUS-X PAN PROFESSIONAL, PLUS-X PAN

Manufacturer: Eastman Kodak

Designation: Amateur (35mm and 70mm long rolls); 4147, Professional (120, 220, sheet film)

Speed: ISO 125

Color sensitivity: Panchromatic

Reciprocity effect: No compensation is required for exposures in 1/10,000 to 1/10 sec. range, although Kodak recommends increasing developing time by 10% for 1/10,000 and 1/1000 sec. exposures. For a 1 second exposure, add 1 stop and reduce developing time by 10%; for a 10 second exposure, add 2 stops and reduce developing time by 20%; for a 100 second exposure, add 3 stops and reduce developing time by 30%.

Grain: Very fine

Degree of enlargement: Very high

Resolving power: 125 lines/mm

Exposure latitue: +/−2 stops

Contrast: Medium

Processing: D-76, 5 1/2 minutes; HC-110 (dilution B), 5 minutes; Microdol-X, 7 minutes.

Push-processing: Not recommended

Format: 35mm, 35mm and 70mm long rolls; Plus-X Pan Professional, 120, 220; 4 × 5, 8 × 10

Uses: A general-purpose medium-speed black-and-white film for portraits, commercial work, and amateur photography.

Comments: The fate of this film was unclear when T-Max 100 was introduced, but its fine grain, forgiving exposure latitude, and overall "look" is still popular. The retouching surface on the pro film's emulsion side is useful for portrait work.

VERICHROME PAN

Manufacturer: Eastman Kodak

Designation: Amateur

Speed: ISO 125

Color sensitivity: Panchromatic

Reciprocity effect: Not available

Grain: Fine

Degree of enlargement: High

Resolving power: 100 lines/mm

Exposure latitude: +/–2 stops

Contrast: Medium

Processing: D-76, 7 minutes; HC-110 (dilution B), 5 minutes; Microdol-X, 9 minutes.

Push-processing: Not recommended

Format: 120

Uses: A general-purpose film for daylight/electronic flash.

Comments: This old standard offers very good tonal gradation and wide exposure latitude, which makes it useful when just the right exposure isn't easy to obtain. For this reason, it is a favorite among photographers who like to shoot with old roll film and box cameras offering little exposure control.

Kodak

Verichrome
pan film

8, 10, 12, OR 16 EXP

VP 120

BLACK-AND-WHITE FILMS

ISO 200

SUPER-XX PAN PROFESSIONAL

Manufacturer: Eastman Kodak

Designation: 4142, Professional

Speed: ISO 200

Color sensitivity: Panchromatic

Reciprocity effect: For exposures in 1/1000 to 1/10 sec. range no compensation is required. Add 1 stop and reduce developing time by 10% for a 1 second exposure; for a 10 second exposure, add 2 stops and reduce developing time by 20%; for a 100 second exposure, add 3 stops and reduce developing time by 30%.

Grain: Fine

Degree of enlargement: Moderate

Resolving power: 100 lines/mm

Exposure latitude: Not available

Contrast: Medium

Processing: HC-110 (dilution B), 5 minutes; DK-50, 4 1/4 minutes.

Push-processing: Not recommended

Format: 4 × 5, 5 × 7, 8 × 10, 10 × 12, 11 × 14

Uses: Though this film can be used for general-purpose photography, it is mainly used for making internegatives from color transparencies; it can also be used for making color separations and dye transfer negatives.

Comments: If you make a black-and-white internegative on conventional black-and-white film, there is a good chance that certain colors won't record properly. Not so with this film, which is designed to produce excellent tonal reproduction from color slides.

AGFAPAN 400 PROFESSIONAL

Manufacturer: Agfa

Designation: Professional

Speed: ISO 400

Color sensitivity: Panchromatic

Reciprocity effect: No compensation required for exposures in 1/10,000 to 1/2 sec. range. Add one stop and reduce developing time by 10% for a 1 second exposure; add 2 1/2 stops and reduce developing time by 25% for a 10 second exposure; add 3 1/2 stops and reduce developing time by 35% for a 100 second exposure.

Grain: Fine

Degree of enlargement: Moderately high

Resolving power: 110 lines/mm

Exposure latitude: +/–2 1/2 stops

Contrast: Medium

Processing: In Agfa-recommended developers at 68-degrees F: Refinal, 6 minutes; Rodinal 1:50, 9 minutes.

Push-processing: Agfa recommends pushing only in Atomal developer, and only when necessary. For an EI 1000, 14 minutes; for EI 1600, 16 minutes.

Format: 35mm, 35mm × 100 ft., 120, 6 × 9cm, 9 × 12cm, 8 × 10

Uses: A medium-fast film for low-light photography and action photography in daylight.

Comments: Agfa's ISO 400 film has very good grain and sharpness for the speed, plus an excellent tonal rendition that appeals to photographers who like a touch of pleasing grain in their images.

BLACK-AND-WHITE FILMS

ISO 400

DELTA 400

Manufacturer: Ilford

Designation: Professional

Speed: ISO 400

Color sensitivity: Panchromatic

Reciprocity effect: No compensation is required for exposures in 1/10,000 to 1/2 sec. range. Test for longer exposures.

Grain: Fine

Degree of enlargement: High

Resolving power. Not available

Exposure latitude: +/–2½ to 3 stops. According to Ilford, quality results can be obtained using exposure ratings in EI 200 to EI 800 range.

Contrast: Medium

Processing: For ISO 400: Ilford Universal, 1:4, 10 minutes; ID-11 Plus, 1:1, 9 minutes; Kodak D-76, 1:1, 9 minutes. For EI 200: Ilford Universal, 1:14, 6 1/2 minutes; ID-11 Plus, 1:1, 8 minutes; Kodak D-76, 1:1, 8 minutes. For EI 800: Ilford Universal, 1:9, 9 minutes; ID-11 Plus, 1:1, 14 minutes; Kodak D-76, 1:1, 14 minutes.

Push-processing: See above for EI 800. For EI 1600, use Microphen stock for 8 minutes. Ilford actually recommends using their HP5-Plus for pushing to this speed and faster.

Format: 35mm, 35mm long roll

Uses: A fast, fine-grain black-and-white film intended for pictorial and fine-art photographers.

Comments: Using new film-building technology, Ilford has introduced an outstandingly sharp, fine-grain, tonally rich new film. Ilford claims that the grain matches that of slower-speed films; thus Delta 400 can be used to gain faster shutter speeds or greater depth of field even in daylight shooting conditions. Ilford is positioning Delta as the 35mm art photographer's film.

ILFORD HP5 PLUS

Manufacturer: Ilford

Designation: Professional

Speed: ISO 400

Color sensitivity: Panchromatic

Reciprocity effect: For exposures between 1/10,000 and 1/2 sec., no compensation is required. For a 1 second exposure, add 1/2 stop; for a 10 second exposure, add 2 stops.

Grain: Fine

Degree of enlargement: Moderately high

Resolving power: Not available

Exposure latitude: +/–2 1/2 stops, plus 1 stop when developed and exposed accordingly.

Contrast: Medium

Processing: D-76, 7 1/2 minutes; T-Max (1:4), 6 1/2 minutes; Microphen, 6 1/2 minutes.

Push-processing: For EI 800: D-76, 9 1/2 minutes; T-Max (1:4), 8 minutes; Microphen, 8 minutes. For EI 1600: D-76, 12 1/2 minutes; T-Max (1:4), 9 1/2 minutes; Microphen, 11 minutes. For EI 3200: T-Max (1:4), 11 1/2 minutes; Microphen, 16 minutes.

Format: 35mm, 35mm long roll (100 ft.), 120, 220, 4 × 5, 8 × 10

Uses: A general-purpose, highly pushable black-and-white film for photojournalism, street photography, and for low-light scenes.

Comments: HP5 Plus is the recent update of the long-standing Ilford HP-5. It has fine grain, very good sharpness, and a wide exposure latitude for shooting under a wide variety of lighting conditions. It pushes extremely well and gives good results in speeds ranging from its rated ISO 400 to EI 1600. Along with the film came a new developer, Ilfotec HC; at a 1:15 dilution developed for 11 minutes it yields a printable EI 3200 negative.

BLACK-AND-WHITE FILMS

ISO 400

DX   135   36

ILFORD XP2 400

Manufacturer: Ilford

Designation: Professional/Amateur

Speed: ISO 400

Color sensitivity: Panchromatic

Grain: Very fine

Degree of enlargement: High

Resolving power: Not available

Exposure latitude: +3/−1 stop

Contrast: Medium

Processing: C-41, XP2 Processing Kit

Push-processing: Not recommended

Format: 35mm, 120, 4 × 5, 8 × 10, 11 × 14

Uses: This fast chromogenic black-and-white film is for general-purpose photography.

Comments: XP2, which replaces XP1, is a unique type of black-and-white film because it uses color dyes rather than silver as the image-forming material. Slight overexposure actually decreases its grain, as dye clouds instead of silver clumps form the image. The film is touted as having a wide exposure latitude. Best quality images are obtained from it at ISO 400; exposure at EI 200 gives finer grain, and EI 50 exposures yield very fine-grain but rather dense negatives. The fastest speed is ISO 800, which increases contrast. Separate frames can be rated at speeds within this range, as the film is processed in a standard C-41 process. XP2 is also good for producing black-and-white internegatives from slides. The convenience of being able to have this film processed and printed in one-hour labs is considered a plus by some photographers.

NEOPAN 400 PROFESSIONAL

Manufacturer: Fuji

Designation: Professional

Speed: ISO 400

Color sensitivity: Panchromatic

Grain: Fine

Degree of enlargement: Moderately high

Resolving power: Not available

Exposure latitude: +/−2 1/2 stops

Contrast: Medium

Processing: D-76, 7 1/2 minutes; T-Max, 6 minutes; Microphen, 4 1/4 minutes; Acufine 3 1/4 minutes.

Push-processing: For EI 800: D-76, 8 3/4 minutes; T-Max, 7 1/2 minutes; Microphen, 5 3/4 minutes; Acufine, 4 1/2 minutes. For EI 1600: D-76, 13 1/2 minutes; T-Max, 10 minutes; Microphen, 8 1/2 minutes; Acufine, 7 minutes.

Format: 35mm, 35mm long roll (100 ft.), 120

Uses: A general-purpose medium-speed black-and-white film for news, sports, and low-light photography.

Comments: A good black-and-white film for general shooting purposes with fine grain and excellent sharpness. It has undergone recent revisions that make it more amenable to push-processing. Another design change that makes this film highly usable in motor-drive transport systems: it is highly resistant to static marks, and is smooth and flexible.

BLACK-AND-WHITE FILMS

ISO 400

T-MAX 400 PROFESSIONAL

Manufacturer: Eastman Kodak

Designation: 5053 (35mm); 6053 (120); 4053 (sheet film); Professional

Speed: ISO 400

Color sensitivity: Panchromatic, with less blue sensitivity than conventional films.

Reciprocity effect: No compensation required for exposures in 1/10,000 to 1/10 sec. range. Add 1/3 stop for 1 second exposure, add 1/2 stop for 10 second exposure; add 1 1/2 stops for 100 second exposure.

Grain: Very fine

Degree of enlargement: High

Resolving power: 125 lines/mm

Exposure latitude: +3/−2 stops

Contrast: Medium

Processing: T-Max developer at 75 degrees F, 6 minutes; D-76 at 68 degrees F, 8 minutes; HC-110 (dilution B) at 68 degrees F, 6 minutes. Tray processing of sheet film: D-76 at 68 degrees F, 7 minutes.

Push-processing: No increase in developing time is required for films exposed at EI 800. For EI 1600: T-Max developer at 75 degrees F, 8 minutes; D-76 at 68 degrees F, 10 1/2 minutes. For EI 3200: T-Max developer at 75 degrees F, 9 1/2 minutes.

Format: 35mm, 35mm and 70mm long rolls, 120, 4 × 5, 5 × 7, 8 × 10

Uses: A general-purpose professional film for low light, fast action, and when high shutter speeds and/or narrow apertures are required.

Comments: The fine grain/fast speed of this film is truly impressive. This film requires critical processing controls, but that care pays excellent dividends.

TRI-X PAN, TRI-X PAN PROFESSIONAL

Manufacturer: Eastman Kodak

Designation: 35mm, 35mm long roll, 120, 220, sheet film sizes

Speed: ISO 400; Professional, ISO 320

Color sensitivity: Panchromatic

Reciprocity effect: No compensation is required for exposures in 1/10,000 to 1/10 sec. range. For a 1 second exposure, add 1 stop and decrease developing time by 10%; for a 10 second exposure, add 2 stops and decrease developing time by 20%.

Grain: Fine

Degree of enlargement: Moderately high

Resolving power: 100 lines/mm

Exposure latitude: +/−2½ stops

Contrast: Medium

Processing: D-76, 8 minutes; HC-110 (dilution B), 7 1/2 minutes; T-Max at 75 degrees F, 5 1/2 minutes. For tray developing of sheet films: D-76, 5 1/2 minutes.

Push-processing: For EI 800, D-76, 11 minutes. For EI 1600: D-76, 13 minutes; HC-110 (dilution B) 16 minutes; T-Max developer at 75 degrees F, 8 minutes. For EI 3200: T-Max developer at 75 degrees F, 11 minutes.

Format: Amateur: 35mm, 35mm long roll; Professional: 120, 220, 4 × 5, 8 × 10

Uses: A general-purpose medium-fast black-and-white film.

Comments: Though Kodak offers a finer-grain ISO 400 film (T-Max 400), many photographers stick with the classic Tri-X because of its pleasing grain structure, wide exposure latitude, forgiveness of exposure miscues, and its overall "look."

ISO 1000

Kodak
**RECORDING
FILM 2475**

36 EXPOSURES
RE 135-36

RECORDING FILM

Manufacturer: Eastman Kodak

Designation: 2475

Speed: EI 1000, can be pushed to EI 3200 and beyond

Color sensitivity: Panchromatic, with extended red sensitivity

Reciprocity effect: For exposures of 1/10 sec. or faster, no compensation is required. Add 2/3 stop for a 1 second exposure; add 1 1/3 stop for a 10 second exposure; add 2 1/3 stop for a 100 second exposure.

Grain: Coarse

Degree of enlargement: Low

Resolving power: 63 lines/mm

Exposure latitude: +/−1 stop

Contrast: Medium; additional contrast as exposure time increases

Processing: HC-110 (diltuion B), 9 minutes for average subjects; HC-110 (dilution B), 15 minutes for low-contrast subjects

Push-processing: Increase processing time by 1/2 for each stop pushed.

Format: 35mm, 35mm long rolls

Uses: A very coarse-grain film for low-light photography, it can also be used for pictorial work where high grain is desired.

Comments: Originally made for surveillance photography, this film can also be used for indoor sports or when a high degree of grain is desired for pictorial effects. The extended red sensivity makes it a good choice for night work. The grain of this film is coarse, but it is often used for special effects.

NEOPAN 1600

Manufacturer: Fuji
Designation: Professional
Speed: ISO 1600
Color sensitivity: Panchromatic
Reciprocity effect: Not available
Grain: Medium
Degree of enlargement: Moderately low
Resolving power: Not available
Exposure latitude: +/−2 stops
Contrast: Medium to medium high
Processing: EI 800: D-76, 5 minutes; EI 1600: D-76, 7 1/2 minutes; T-Max, 4 1/2 minutes; Microphen, 3 1/4 minutes.

Push-processing: EI 3200: D-76, 15 minutes; T-Max, 10 minutes; Microphen, 5 3/4 minutes.

Format: 35mm, 35mm long roll (100 ft.)

Uses: A fast black-and-white film for news, sports, and general photography in low-light conditions.

Comments: This highly versatile, fast film offers short developing times for ratings in the EI 800 to 3200 range. Formulated for motor-drive handling, it is resistant to static marks and moves smoothly through the rigors of fast transport. Neopan 1600 has good grain and contrast for the speed.

BLACK-AND-WHITE FILMS

ISO 3200

T-MAX P3200 PROFESSIONAL

Manufacturer: Eastman Kodak

Designation: 5054, Professional

Speed: ISO 3200

Color sensitivity: Panchromatic, with less blue sensitivity than conventional films

Reciprocity effect: No compensation is required for exposures in 1/10,000 to 1 second range. Add 2/3 stop for 10 second exposures.

Grain: Fine (for speed)

Degree of enlargement: Moderately low

Resolving power: 125 lines/mm

Exposure latitude: +2/−1 stop

Contrast: Medium

Processing: In T-Max developer at 75 degrees F: for EI 400, 6 minutes; for EI 800, 6 1/2 minutes; for EI 1600, 7 minutes; for EI 3200, 9 1/2 minutes; for EI 6400, 11 minutes; for EI 12,500, 12 1/2 minutes; for EI 25,000, 14 minutes.

Push-processing: See above

Format: 35mm

Uses: A very versatile film made for pushing to extended speed ratings. For fast action, low light, handheld telephoto lenses for sports, and when a fast shutter speed/narrow aperture is required, it can be processed for a wide range of speeds.

Comments: Kodak has applied T-grain technology to a highly pushable film. The result is fine grain for the speed at ratings as high as EI 12,500. Note that this film is extremely sensitive to environmental radiation, and must be exposed and processed promptly, and subject to only visual inspection at airports. When pushed to high speeds, this film really shows its stuff.

PROFESSIONAL COPY FILM

Manufacturer: Eastman Kodak

Designation: 4125, Professional

Speed: Variable. With white-flame arc, EI 25; with tungsten and quartz iodine, EI 12; with pulsed xenon, EI 25.

Color sensitivity: Orthochromatic

Reciprocity effect: See packaged instructions.

Grain: Fine

Degree of enlargement: Moderate

Resolving power: 80 lines/mm

Contrast: Highlight contrast is controlled through exposure. Increased exposure increases highlight contrast and negative density range; decreased exposure reduces highlight contrast and negative density range.

Processing: Tray: HC-110 (dilution E), 4 minutes.

Push-processing: Not recommended

Format: 4 × 5, 5 × 7, 8 × 10, 10 × 12, 11 × 14, 20 × 24, 9 × 12cm

Uses: A film designed for copying continuous-tone original photographs.

Comments: If you have a great black-and-white print that took lots of handwork and you want to copy it rather than go through the same work again, this is the film for you. It is specially designed to capture all the nuances and tones of originals, avoiding the flat look of copies made from conventional camera films. Contrast can be varied by exposure.

BLACK-AND-WHITE FILMS

SPECIAL PURPOSE

Kodak
High Speed Infrared Film

36 EXPOSURES
HIE 135-36

HIGH-SPEED INFRARED

Manufacturer: Eastman Kodak

Designation: Amateur

Speed: Because of nature of infrared films, Kodak recommends bracketing several stops from "conventional" exposures. Many photographers start with a speed of EI 125. See comments below.

Color sensitivity: Infrared

Grain: Moderately fine

Degree of enlargement: Moderately low

Resolving power: 80 lines/mm

Exposure latitude: Does not apply. See note below.

Contrast: Medium to medium high

Processing: For pictorial use, D-76, 9 1/2 minutes at 68 degrees F

Push-processing: Not recommended

Uses: A versatile infrared-sensitive film for technical and pictorial photography.

Format: 35mm

Comments: This is one of the cult-status films that falls in and out of favor with pictorial photographers. Because the ratio of infrared radiation to visible light varies, exact speed ratings aren't published. Kodak recommends bracketing exposures under all conditions. For general photography, a #25 filter (red) is recommended. Note: Infrared film has a different focusing point from conventional films. Many lenses have a small red dot on the barrel to indicate the focusing point for this film. To minimize fogging, load film in total darkness and process as soon as possible after exposure.

INSTANT FILMS

INSTANT COLOR PRINT FILMS

ISO 80

Types 668, 58, 808 Polacolor 2
Types 669, 108, 88, 59, 559,
559 Silk, 809 Polacolor ER

ISO 100

Type 660 Polacolor EB

ISO 150

Time Zero Supercolor

ISO 600

Spectra, 600 Plus

INSTANT TRANSPARENCY FILMS

ISO 8

PolaBlue

ISO 40

Polachrome CS, HC

ISO 125

Polapan CT

ISO 400

Polagraph HC

INSTANT BLACK-AND-WHITE PRINT FILMS

ISO 50

Type 55 Positive/Negative

ISO 75

Type 665 Positive/Negative

ISO 100

Types 664, 554, 54, 804

ISO 200

Types 661, 811

ISO 320

Type 51

ISO 400

Types 52, 552 Polapan

ISO 800

Types 53, 553, 803

ISO 3000

Type 87
Types 107, 084, 57
Types 107C, 667

In 1948, Edwin Land launched the Polaroid Land film system that produced a sepia-toned positive print in 60 seconds. Since then, Polaroid has become a household word for "instant" photography. The range of Polaroid products, with many matched to very specific shooting needs, is impressive.

Polaroid instant films differ from conventional print and transparency films in that the developer is either incorporated in the film pack as a pod or, in the case of the 35mm instant slide films, is introduced by a separate developer pack containing a strip that couples to the film within Polaroid's Autoprocessing unit. In each case, the developing agent is spread or diffused within the film emulsion via pressure rollers. This requires specially built cameras or film backs for conventional cameras; as mentioned, the slide film requires a dedicated self-processing unit. The attraction to and usefulness of Polaroid photography is the quick images it affords.

In peel-apart Polaroid films, the image is formed when unexposed silver halide grains from the processed film migrate to a receiving sheet that becomes the positive; the negative image is peeled away. (In the case of positive/negative-type film, a printable negative is also obtained.) Some of these films require the addition of a stabilizer after processing; others do not. The former are referred to as films "requiring coating"; the latter are called "coaterless." With integral films, such as films for the Spectra camera, the developing process takes place within a coated overlayer where dyes form a positive image—no peel-apart sheet is used.

Instant slides work in a similar fashion to peel-apart films, in that the unexposed silver halide forms the image. With instant color-slide films, the colors are formed by a permanent color filter layer unaffected by exposure. Color is determined by the metallic silver density that underlies the tiny strips of color filters, rather than with dyes. In many ways, this additive color system resembles the one used with Autochrome films of years past.

For the most part, the specifications listed for instant films are similar to the previous listings. The exceptions are as follows:

The categories "Designation," "Degree of enlargement," and "Push-processing" have been deleted. "Designation" has been dropped because these films are used for various purposes by both amateurs and professionals. For example, users may work with a Polaroid camera to document damage to a vehicle for insurance purposes at the office, then use the same camera and film to photograph a birthday party at home. In fact, the only Polaroid products specifically designated as "Amateur" are a handful of eight-exposure pack films. The "Degree of enlargement" has been deleted since the end product of these films is instant prints. The fact that the end product is prints means the exposure latitude is necessarily narrow; therefore, correct exposure of most Polaroid materials is crucial. Also, there is no "Push-processing" listing, for obvious reasons.

Keep in mind that resolution figures for prints (the end product of the majority of Polaroid products) will be quite a bit lower than for film measurements. Each film's "resolving power" is given to allow you to compare one Polaroid product to another.

In the same vein, contrast with conventional black-and-white films can be adjusted during development, as well as when prints are made. With Polaroid films, contrast is determined more by film selection, although some latitude can be gained by varying temperature and developing time and using contrast-enhancing filters over the camera lens during exposure.

The Polaroid instant films in this book are broken into three groups: Instant Color Print Films, Instant Transparency Films, and Instant Black-and-White Print Films. Within each group, films are listed according to their approximate film speed. All of these products are for general photographic purposes; films for medical, scientific, or esoteric usage are not included.

Be aware that Polaroid films are made for a number of different formats, backs, and specifically dedicated cameras. The listings here include the following formats:

Polaroid Roll Films. Made for the original 3 1/4 × 4 1/4 cameras and some accessory backs, these are eight-exposure peel-apart rolls that deliver a 2 7/8 × 3 3/4-inch image size. The manufacture of cameras and backs for this film have been discontinued for some time, but many are still in use.

Polaroid Pack Films. These eight-exposure 3 1/4 × 4 1/4 format packs are used for general and professional photography. Polaroid produced a number of cameras for this format, plus there are a myriad of specially built backs for cameras of all types. These peel-apart films are often used on camera backs by professional photographers for testing lighting balance and final shot setup before exposing conventional film.

Polaroid 4 × 5 Single Exposure Packs. Introduced in 1958, 4 × 5 film packets allow photographers with 4 × 5 equipment to use Polaroid film. The current film holder is the 545, which can be used with most cameras that accept standard 4 × 5 sheet film holders, as well as on various types of instruments and custom-built-equipment. In general, these packs are sold 20 to a box and are peel-apart films.

Polaroid 4 × 5 Pack Films. These films are designed for use with a Model 550 film holder on most 4 × 5 cameras, on Polaroid MP-4 camera systems, and with other 4 × 5 equipment designed for the holder. These peel-apart films come eight to a pack.

Polaroid 8 × 10 Films. The magic of an instant 8 × 10 print can't be denied. These large-format films use a special film holder and motorized processor. After exposure, a positive print sheet is loaded into the holder and the package is inserted into a dedicated processor.

Polaroid Integral Films. Today's buyer of Polaroid amateur cameras use many of these films. By "integral," Polaroid means a self-contained product that requires no timing or peeling for the finished print. All components—the negative, positive, and chemical pod—are in each film packet.

Polaroid Instant Slide Films. Designed for use with 35mm cameras, Polaroid Instant Slide Films provide quick access to color, continuous tone black and white, and high-contrast black-and-white and blue-line film for title slides and graphic presentations.

TYPES 668, 58, 808 POLACOLOR 2

Manufacturer: Polaroid

Speed: Equivalent to ISO 80

Balanced for: Daylight/electronic flash

Reciprocity effect: For flash exposure at 1/1000 sec. and daylight exposure at 1/125 sec., no compensation is required. For flash exposure faster than 1/1000 sec., add a CC10B filter. For a daylight exposure of 1/8 sec., add a CC10Y filter. For a daylight exposure of 1 second add a CC30R+CC40Y filter and adjust meter for the filter factor.

Grain: Medium

Resolving power: 18 lines/mm

Color rendition: Rich, saturated color

Exposure latitude: Narrow

Contrast: Medium to medium high

Processing: Normal processing for a temperature range of 70 to 85 degrees F is 60 seconds. At 85 to 90 degrees F, subtract 1/2 stop. At 60 to 70 degrees F, develop for 75 seconds and add 1/2 stop. Development begins when the film is drawn from the camera or back, except with Type 808 8 × 10 film, which requires a special processing setup.

Format: Type 668, 3 1/4 × 4 1/4 in Pack film, 8 exposures per pack; Type 58, 4 × 5 Single Pack Film; Type 808, 8 × 10 sheet film.

Uses: For instant prints where slight color contrast enhancement is required.

Comments: Polacolor 2's slightly higher color contrast rendition makes for snappier pictures when contrast is needed to bring out details or when "hotter" colors are desired. As such, it can be used as an alternative to Types 108 and 669 films.

Polaroid
Polacolor Instant Pack Film.
108

TYPES 669, 108, 88, 59, 559, 559 SILK, 809 POLACOLOR ER

Manufacturer: Polaroid

Speed: Equivalent to ISO 80

Balanced for: Daylight/electronic flash

Reciprocity effect: For flash exposures at or above 1/3000 sec., add a CC10C filter. No compensation is required for flash exposures at 1/1000 or daylight exposures at 1/125 sec. Add a CC05R filter for flash exposures at 1/30 sec. For daylight exposure at 1/4 sec., add a CC20R+CC10Y filter. For a 1 second exposure, add a CC30R+CC10Y filter. Adjust ISO for filter factors accordingly.

Grain: Medium

Resolving power: 14 lines/mm

Color rendition: Rich, saturated colors

Exposure latitude: Narrow

Contrast: Medium

Processing: At 90 degrees F, develop for 60 seconds, and subtract 1/3 stop. At 75 degrees F, develop for 60 seconds. At 65 degrees F, develop for 75 seconds and add 1/2 stop. At 55 degrees F, develop for 90 seconds and add 1 stop.

Format: Type 669/108/88, Pack film, 8 exposures per pack. Type 88 image size: 2 3/4 × 2 7/8 inches. Type 59, 4 × 5 Single Exposure Packs; Type 559 and Type 559 Silk, 4 × 5 Pack Films; Type 809, 8 × 10.

Uses: Medium-speed instant color print films for general photography.

Comments: "ER" for "extended range," means the film records rich shadow and delicate highlight detail, and can capture relatively wide ranges of scene brightness.

TYPE 660
POLACOLOR EB

Manufacturer: Polaroid

Speed: ISO 100

Balanced for: Daylight/electronic flash

Reciprocity: No compensation is required for daylight/electronic flash exposures at 1/30 sec. or less. Add a CC20M filter and reduce ISO to 80 for a 1/4 or 1/8 sec. exposure time. For a 1 second exposure, add a CC20M and CC10B filter and set ISO to 50. For a 10 second exposure, add a CC20M and CC30B filter and set ISO at 12.

Grain: Medium

Resolving power: Not available

Color rendition: Rich, saturated colors

Exposure latitude: Narrow

Contrast: Medium

Processing: Best results are obtained at 75 degrees F to 95 degrees F; process for 90 seconds. At 65 degrees F, process for 120 seconds. At 55 degrees F, process for 180 seconds. Development begins when the film is withdrawn from the camera or back.

Format: Pack film, 8 exposures per pack; image size 2 7/8 × 3 3/4 inches

Uses: Yields positive color prints for cameras and camera backs that accept Polaroid Pack films.

Comments: This recently introduced film bears the "EB" Polaroid moniker, meaning "enhanced brightness." Type 660 has a slightly higher speed than Type 668 (see listing) and higher, more vivid color saturation. It also has an expanded "recommended" temperature range for processing.

TIME ZERO SUPERCOLOR

Manufacturer: Polaroid

Speed: Approximately ISO 150

Balanced for: Daylight/electronic flash

Reciprocity: Not available

Grain: Medium

Resolving power: 10 lines/mm

Color rendition: Rich, saturated colors

Exposure latitude: Narrow

Contrast: Medium

Processing: Self-processing, begins upon ejection from camera. Recommended temperature for processing is 70 degrees F and above. At 55 degrees F, speed or color balance may be affected.

Format: 3 1/2 × 4 1/4 inches, ten exposures per pack; image size 3 1/8 × 3 1/8 inches

Uses: Positive color-print film for cameras that use Time Zero film.

Comments: This self-developing film for amateur Polaroid cameras delivers a glossy, color-rich rendition of scenic, family, and vacation photos.

SPECTRA, 600 PLUS

Manufacturer: Polaroid

Speed: Equivalent to ISO 600

Balanced for: Daylight/electronic flash

Reciprocity: Not available

Grain: Medium

Resolving power: Not available

Color rendition: Rich, saturated colors

Exposure latitude: Narrow

Contrast: Medium

Processing: Self-processing, begins upon ejection from camera. At 55 degrees F, speed or color balance may be affected.

Format: Spectra, print size, 4 × 4 1/16 inches, ten exposures per pack; image area 3 9/16 × 2 7/8 inches. 600 Plus, 3 1/2 × 4 1/2, ten exposures per pack; image area 3 1/8 × 3 1/8 inches.

Uses: A color-positive print film for use in Polaroid amateur cameras and backs that use such film.

Comments: The relatively new Spectra system from Polaroid comes with a new film formulation. The prints it produces are not as glossy as with Supercolor, and Spectra prints have a "luster" finish. Each film pack has a built-in battery that handles camera functions. The Type 600 Plus film is the Spectra film formulation for Polaroid amateur cameras that produces square images.

POLABLUE

Manufacturer: Polaroid

Speed: Daylight, ISO 8; tungsten, ISO 4

Color sensitivity: Orthochromatic

Reciprocity: If exposure is 10 seconds or longer, compensation is required. For a 10 second exposure, open lens 1/2 stop and use a 15 second exposure time. For a 100 second exposure, add 1 stop and increase exposure to 3 minutes.

Grain: Fine

Resolving power: 90 lines/mm

Exposure latitude: Narrow

Contrast: High

Processing: 4 minutes in dedicated Polaroid Autoprocessor. Develop in 65 to 85 degree F range.

Format: 35mm cartridges, 12 exposure load

Uses: A quick-access slide film that yields a negative white-on-blue background image intended for charts, graphs, and typeset graphic material.

Comments: This film is essentially for making quick-access presentation slides for business and institutional applications. Unlike the other Polaroid 35mm instant slide films, it yields a negative image. For example, PolaBlue can be used to make a slide showing white type on a blue background by photographing a typewritten page. Use it with manual-exposure 35mm cameras and handheld meters only.

POLACHROME CS, HC

Manufacturer: Polaroid

Speed: ISO 40

Balanced for: Daylight/electronic flash

Reciprocity effect: No compensation required
for exposures longer than 1/15 sec. Add 1/3 stop
for an 1/8 sec. exposure; add 2/3 stop for a
1/4 sec. exposure; add 1 stop for a 1/2 or 1 second
exposure; add 1 2/3 stop for a 4 second exposure;
add 2 1/3 stop for a 16 second exposure.

Grain: Coarse. Color is formed by filter stripes
built into emulsion; viewing on lightbox or
enlarging film on prints reveals these stripes.

Resolving power: 90 lines/mm

Color rendition: Colors may seem slightly
magenta or odd when viewed on lightbox, but
the film is intended for projection. In projection,
colors are neutral to rich.

Exposure latitude: +/–$\frac{1}{2}$ stop

Contrast: Medium

Processing: At 70 degrees F and above, 60 seconds;
at lower temperatures 2 minutes in dedicated
Polaroid Autoprocessor. Longer times don't affect
results; shorter times can result in poor quality. Best
results are in 65 to 80 degree F range. Develop
Polachrome HC for 2 minutes.

Format: 35mm cartridge. Polachrome CS comes in
12 or 36 exposure lengths; Polachrome HC comes
in 12 exposure lengths.

Uses: For quick access to 35mm color transparencies
for projection presentations, tests, and other general
photographic uses.

Comments: Polachrome HC is the high-contrast
version of Polachrome CS. Due to the nature of
this film's construction, use a handheld meter
when making exposures with an off-the-film plane
metering system.

Polaroid
*High Contrast
PolaChrome 35mm*
Instant Color Slide Film.
Processing pack included.
HCP-135-12. ISO 40/17°
For professional use.

SALES
BY REGION

Polaroid
PolaPan 35mm
Instant Black and White Slide Film.
Continuous tone.
Processing pack included.
CT-135-12. ISO 125/22°
For professional use.

POLAPAN CT

Manufacturer: Polaroid

Speed: Daylight, ISO 125; tungsten, ISO 80

Color sensitivity: Panchromatic

Reciprocity: No compensation is required for exposures in 1/10,000 to 1/15 sec. range. Add 1/3 stop for a 1/8 sec. exposure time; add 2/3 stop for a 1/4 sec. exposure time; add 1 stop for a 1/2 or 1 second exposure time; add 1 1/3 stop for a 2 second exposure time; add 1 2/3 stop for a 4 second exposure time.

Grain: Fine

Resolving power: 90 lines/mm

Exposure latitude: +2/−1 stop

Contrast: Medium

Processing: At temperatures at or above 70 degrees F, process for 60 seconds in a dedicated Polaroid Autoprocessor. Below 70 degrees F, process for 2 minutes. Best range for processing is 65 to 80 degrees F. Lengthening processing time has no ill effects on results; shortening time may cause quality loss.

Format: 35mm cartridges, 12 or 36 exposure loads

Uses: For quick access to transparencies for continuous-tone rendition of illustrations, photographs, artwork, and other copy material, or for general photography.

Comments: This unique black-and-white slide film can be used for copying monochrome images for presentations. It can also be used as an intermediary step for other photographic and/or graphic processes. As with all instant slide films, the emulsion is delicate, and mounting the slides in glass is recommended for projection. Using a handheld meter when shooting with cameras that have off-the-film-plane metering is recommended. Polapan has less underexposure latitude than conventional slide film.

POLAGRAPH HC

Manufacturer: Polaroid

Speed: Daylight, ISO 400; tungsten, ISO 320

Color sensitivity: Panchromatic

Reciprocity effect: For bright whites: no compensation is required for exposures in 1/10,000 to 1/4 sec. range. Add 1/2 sec. to 1/4 sec. exposure time; add 1 second to 1/2 sec. exposure time; add 3 seconds to 1 second exposure time; add 8 seconds to 2 second exposure time; add 24 seconds to 4 second exposure time. For more continuous-tone results, see reciprocity effect under Polapan listing.

Grain: Fine

Resolving power: 90 lines/mm

Exposure latitude: +2/–1 stop

Contrast: High

Processing: 2 minutes in a dedicated Polaroid Autoprocessor. Recommended processing temperature is 70 degrees F, though a range of 65 to 80 degrees F is tolerable. Lengthening the processing time is no problem, though any shorter time can result in loss of quality.

Format: 35mm cartridge, 12 exposure load

Uses: For quick-access high-contrast black-and-white transparencies of line art, graphs and charts for presentations, and for quick-access high-contrast slides for pictorial and graphic special effects.

Comments: This film yields a positive image of graphs and charts and is used to create quick slides for presentations. However, the film is also used by photographers for high-contrast images and by graphic artists as intermediate film for various conversions and line work. For general purposes, it can be underexposed to render more of a gray scale. Due to the nature of the film's construction, use a handheld meter when shooting it in cameras that have off-the-film-plane metering systems.

Polaroid
PolaGraph 35mm
Instant Black and White Slide Film.
High contrast.
Processing pack included.
HC-135-12. ISO 400/27°
For professional use.

TYPE 55
POSITIVE/NEGATIVE

Manufacturer: Polaroid

Speed: Approximately equivalent to ISO 50

Color sensitivity: Panchromatic

Reciprocity effect: No compensation is required for exposures in 1/1000 to 1 second range. Add 1/3 stop and 3 seconds for a 10 second exposure. Add 1 stop and 100 second for a 100 second exposure.

Grain: Medium

Resolving power: 25 lines/mm on print; 160 lines/mm on negative.

Exposure latitude: Narrow

Contrast: Medium

Processing: At 70 degrees F, develop for 20 seconds. At 65 degrees F, develop for 35 seconds. At 60 degrees F, develop for 40 seconds. At 50 degrees F, develop for 60 seconds. Development begins when film is drawn from holder. Prints must be coated. For negative, within 3 minutes after separation from positive immerse negative and agitate continuously in an 18% sodium sulfite solution. To make, add 440 grams of sodium sulfite in 2 liters of water.

Format: 4 × 5 film packet; image size 3 1/2 × 4 1/2 inches

Uses: When a paper positive print and permanent negative are desired.

Comments: Slightly slower in speed than Type 665 pack film, this 4 × 5 packet film is used extensively for copy work, field shooting, and general professional work where both a paper print and a negative are desired. Follow the negative-clearing instructions carefully. Some photographers also use a hardening bath after clearing to protect the negative's emulsion.

TYPE 665
POSITIVE/NEGATIVE

Manufacturer: Polaroid

Speed: Equivalent to ISO 75

Color sensitivity: Panchromatic

Reciprocity effect: No compensation required for exposures in 1/1000 to 1 second range. Add 1/2 stop and 5 seconds for a 1 second exposure; add 1 1/3 stop and 150 seconds for a 100 second exposure. When shooting in tungsten light, reduce ISO by 1/3.

Grain: Medium

Resolving power: Positive print: 20 lines/mm; negative: 180 lines/mm

Exposure latitude: Narrow

Contrast: Medium

Processing: At 70 degrees F, 30 seconds; at 60 degrees F, 40 seconds; at 50 degrees F, 50 seconds. To clear negative, within 3 minutes after separation from positive, immerse negative with continuous agitation in a 12% solution of sodium sulfite (2 liters of water: 270 grams of sodium sulfite.) Print must be coated.

Format: Pack film, 8 exposures per pack; image size 2 7/8 × 3 3/4 inches

Uses: For general photographic applications when a medium-contrast print and a permanent negative are required.

Comments: Type 665 is used extensively by professional photographers to simultaneously provide a highly printable negative and positive print. This film is used for copy work, by art photographers in the field, and by those who want to see immediate results plus have a negative at the same time. Follow instructions on clearing negative carefully.

INSTANT BLACK-AND-WHITE FILMS

ISO 100

TYPES 664, 554, 54, 804

Manufacturer: Polaroid

Speed: Daylight, ISO 100; Tungsten, ISO 64

Color sensitivity: Panchromatic

Reciprocity effect: Intended for exposures of 1/10 sec. or faster. No compensation is required for exposures in 1/1000 to 1/10 sec. range.

Grain: Fine

Resolving power: 25 lines/mm

Exposure latitude: Narrow

Contrast: Medium

Processing: 30 seconds at 75 degrees F. At 65 degrees F, process for 60 seconds. At 60 degrees F, lower EI to 64 for daylight and EI 40 for tungsten and process for 75 seconds. Processing begins when the film is drawn from the camera or back, except with 8 × 10 film, which requires a dedicated processing setup. Coaterless.

Format: Type 664 is 8-exposure pack film; Type 554 is 4 × 5 Pack film; Type 54 is 4 × 5 Single Exposure Packet; Type 804 is Polaroid 8 × 10 film.

Uses: An instant black-and-white print film that is speed-matched to many popular professional chrome films; ideal for testing.

Comments: This recently introduced film caters to professionals who use Polaroid film extensively for testing and who demanded a film more precisely speed-matched to popular chrome films. Test films can help photographers make judgments about lighting and composition.

TYPES 661, 811

Manufacturer: Polaroid

Speed: Equivalent to ISO 200

Color sensitivity: Panchromatic

Reciprocity effect: No compensation is required for exposures in 1/1000 to 1 second range. Add 1/3 stop and 13 seconds for a 10 second exposure; add 1 stop and 200 seconds for a 100 second exposure.

Grain: Medium

Resolving power: 20 lines/mm

Exposure latitude: Narrow

Contrast: Low

Processing: 45 seconds at 65 to 75 degrees F. Processing times up to 3 minutes won't affect results. Processing begins after film is drawn from back; for 8 × 10 format the dedicated Polaroid processor is required. Coaterless.

Format: Type 811, 8 × 10; type 611, 3 1/4 × 4 1/4 pack film

Uses: Intended for video image recording.

Comments: This low-contrast film offers an extended gray-scale recording capability and is designed for producing a full range of densities from a video monitor. It isn't recommended for general photography.

TYPE 51

Manufacturer: Polaroid

Speed: Daylight, equivalent to ISO 320; tungsten, equivalent to ISO 125

Color sensitivity: Blue sensitive

Reciprocity effect: No compensation required for exposures in 1/1000 to 1/10 sec. range. Add 1/3 stop for a 1 second exposure. Add 2/3 stop and 6 seconds for a 10 second exposure. Add 1 1/3 stop and 150 seconds for a 150 second exposure.

Grain: Medium

Resolving power: 32 lines/mm

Exposure latitude: Narrow

Contrast: High

Processing: At temperatures of 65 degrees F, process for 15 to 20 seconds for line art, 10 seconds for halftones. At temperatures of 60 degrees F and below, process for 20 to 25 seconds for line art, 10 seconds for halftones. Development begins when film is drawn from holder. Prints must be coated.

Format: 4 × 5 film packet; image size: 3 1/2 × 4 1/2 inches

Uses: For high-contrast paper-print positives.

Comments: This blue-sensitive print film is ideal for graphic arts and halftone applications, plus it can be used for photomicography and laboratory sciences. Photographers also use it for in-camera graphic renditions of general subject matter.

TYPES 52, 552 POLAPAN

Polaroid
PolaPan 4x5 Instant Pack Film.
Medium contrast.
8 black and white prints.
4x5 in. (9x12 cm).
ISO 400/27°
For professional use.

Manufacturer: Polaroid

Speed: Equivalent to ISO 400

Color sensitivity: Panchromatic

Reciprocity effect: No compensation required for exposures in 1/1000 to 1 second range. Add 1/3 stop and 3 seconds for a 10 second exposure. Add 1 stop and 100 seconds for a 100 second exposure. When exposing under tungsten light, reduce ISO by 1/3 stop.

Grain: Medium fine

Resolving power: 25 lines/mm

Exposure latitude: Narrow

Contrast: Medium

Processing: For temperatures of 75 degrees F and above, develop for 20 seconds. At 70 degrees F, develop for 25 seconds. At 65 degrees F, develop for 30 seconds. At 60 degrees F, develop for 35 to 40 seconds. At 50 degrees F, develop for 50 to 55 seconds. Prints must be coated.

Format: Type 52, 4 × 5 film packet; image size 3 1/2 × 4 1/2 inches; Type 552, 4 × 5 Pack film, 8 exposures per pack.

Uses: For medium-contrast paper-positive prints. Suited for general-purpose photography.

Comments: This relatively fine-grain, medium-fast print film delivers excellent tonal rendition and can be used for a wide range of professional applications. Speed-matching is very close to ISO 400 black-and-white films, thus Polapan is often used for testing. Note that speed is given as "equivalent to ISO 400," so testing to match developing technique and conventional film speed with Polapan is a must.

TYPES 53, 553, 803

Manufacturer: Polaroid

Speed: Equivalent to ISO 800

Color sensitivity: Panchromatic

Reciprocity effect: No compensation is required for exposures in 1/1000 to 1/10 sec. range. Add 1/3 stop for a 1 second exposure. Add 2/3 stop and 8 seconds for a 10 second exposure. Add 1 2/3 stop and 220 seconds for a 100 second exposure. Reduce ISO by 1/3 stop when exposing under tungsten lights.

Grain: Medium

Resolving power: 22 lines/mm

Exposure latitude: Narrow

Contrast: Medium to medium high

Processing: At 75 degrees F, develop for 30 seconds. At 70 degrees F, develop for 45 seconds. At 65 degrees F, develop for 60 seconds. At 60 degrees F, develop for 75 seconds. At 50 degrees F, develop for 90 seconds. Development begins when film is drawn from holder. Coaterless. Type 83 is 8 × 10 film and must be processed using dedicated Polaroid 8 × 10 processor.

Format: Type 53, 4 × 5 film packet; image size 3 1/2 × 4 1/2 inches; Type 553, 4 × 5 Pack film, 8 exposures per pack; Type 803, 8 × 10 sheet film.

Uses: Designed for high-volume scientific purposes—especially electron microscopy—and other professional applications where coating may be inconvenient.

Comments: This fast black-and-white print film produces higher-contrast images than type 52 film. The film has very clean whites and a lustrous surface texture. Though aimed primarily at the scientific community, commercial and pictorial photographers have also discovered this film's charms.

TYPE 87

ISO 3000

Manufacturer: Polaroid

Speed: Equivalent to ISO 3000

Color sensitivity: Panchromatic

Reciprocity effect: No compensation is required for exposures in 1/1000 to 1/100 sec. range. Add 1/3 stop for a 1/10 sec. exposure; add 2/3 stop and 1 second for a 1 second exposure; add 1 stop and 10 seconds for a 10 second exposure; add 1 2/3 stop and 220 seconds for a 100 second exposure. In tungsten light take off 1/3 stop from speed rating.

Grain: Medium

Resolving power: 20 lines/mm

Exposure latitude: Narrow

Contrast: Medium

Processing: At 75 degrees F and above, process for 30 seconds; for 65 degrees F, process for 60 seconds. Processing begins once film is pulled from camera. Coaterless.

Format: Pack film, 8 exposures per pack; image size 2 3/4 × 2 7/8 inches

Uses: For use in pack cameras or pack film backs. Very high speed for general-purpose photography, for recording high-speed events, and when working in dim lighting conditions.

Comments: This square-format, high-speed film, first introduced in 1971, is for use with Polaroid cameras that make square-format pictures and Model CB80 square-format film backs used on instrumentation and other equipment.

TYPES 107, 084, 57

Manufacturer: Polaroid

Speed: Equivalent to ISO 3000

Color sensitivity: Panchromatic

Reciprocity effect: No compensation is required for exposures in 1/1000 to 1/10 sec. range. Add 1/2 stop and 1/2 sec. for 1 second exposures; add 1 stop and 10 seconds for 10 second exposures; add 1 1/2 stop and 180 seconds for 100 second exposure.

Grain: Medium

Resolving power: 22 lines/mm

Exposure latitude: Narrow

Contrast: Medium

Processing: Normal processing is at 70 degrees F and above for 15 seconds. At 65 degrees F, process for 20 seconds. Development begins when film is pulled from camera or back. Prints must be coated.

Format: Type 107/084, film pack, 8 exposures per pack; Type 57, 4 × 5 single exposure pack.

Uses: A fast film for recording high speed events or when working in dim light.

Comments: Type 084 is the "professional" version of Type 107 pack film, designed for minimum variation and for maximum image quality. It is often used for recording CRT displays. Type 57 has similar specifications and is used with the Model 545 holder or custom-built backs for single-sheet 4 × 5 film packet.

TYPES 107C, 667

Manufacturer: Polaroid

Speed: Equivalent to ISO 3000

Color sensitivity: Panchromatic

Reciprocity effect: No compensation is required for exposures in 1/1000 to 1/10 sec. range. Add 1/3 stop for a 1 second exposure; add 2/3 stop and 8 seconds for a 10 second exposure; add 1 2/3 stop and 220 seconds for a 100 second exposure.

Grain: Medium

Resolving power: 14 lines/mm

Exposure latitude: Narrow

Contrast: Medium

Processing: Normal processing, defined as 75 degrees F, is 30 seconds. At 65 degrees F, process for 60 seconds. Processing begins when the film is drawn out of the camera. Coaterless.

Format: Film pack, 8 exposures; image size 2 7/8 × 3 3/4 inches

Uses: High speed is ideal for general-purpose photography, for high-speed action, and working in dim light.

Comments: Type 667 is the professional version of Type 107C, which in Polaroid parlance means a firm speed rating and maximum image quality. Type 667 is often chosen for biomedical and diagnostic photography.

LIST OF MANUFACTURERS AND THEIR FILMS

AGFA CORPORATION
100 Challenger Road
Ridgefield, New Jersey 07660
(201) 440-2500

Agfachrome 50 RS Professional
Agfachrome CT 100
Agfachrome 100 RS Professional
Agfachrome CT 200
Agfachrome 200 RS Professional
Agfachrome 1000 RS
  Professional
Agfacolor Optima 125
Agfacolor Portrait 160
Agfacolor Ultra 50 Professional
Agfacolor XRG 100
Agfacolor XRS 100 Professional
Agfacolor XRG 200
Agfacolor XRS 200 Professional
Agfacolor XRG 400
Agfacolor XRS 400 Professional
Agfacolor XRS 1000 Professional
Agfaortho 25 Professional
Agfapan 400 Professional
Agfapan APX 25 Professional
Agfapan APX 100 Professional

EASTMAN KODAK COMPANY
343 State Street
Rochester, New York 14650
(716) 724-4000

Ektachrome 50 HC
Ektachrome 50 Professional
Ektachrome 64 Professional
Ektachrome 64 Professional
  EPV
Ektachrome 64 Professional
  EPX
Ektachrome 64T Professional
Ektachrome 100 HC
Ektachrome 100 Plus
  Professional
Ektachrome 100 Professional
Ektachrome 160 Professional,
  160 Amateur
Ektachrome 200 Professional,
  200 Amateur
Ektachrome 400
Ektachrome P800, 1600
  Professional
Ektachrome Duplicating Films
Ektapan
Ektapress Gold 100
Ektapress Gold 400
Ektapress Gold 1600
Ektar 25, Ektar 25 Professional
Ektar 125
Ektar 1000
High-Speed Infrared
Kodachrome 25 Professional, 25
  Amateur
Kodachrome 40 Type A
  Professional

Kodachrome 64 Professional,
64 Amateur
Kodachrome 200 Professional,
200 Amateur
Kodacolor Gold 100
Kodacolor Gold 200
Kodacolor Gold 1600
Kodak Gold 400
Plus-X Pan Professional, Plus-X
Pan
Professional Copy Film
Recording Film
Super-XX Pan Professional
T-Max 100
T-Max 400 Professional
T-Max P3200 Professional
Tri-X Pan, Tri-X Pan Professional
Technical Pan
Verichrome Pan
Vericolor HC Professional
Vericolor Slide Film
Vericolor III Professional
Vericolor 400

Fujichrome P1600
Professional D
Fujichrome Velvia
Fujicolor 160 Professional L
Fujicolor Professional S
Fujicolor Reala
Fujicolor Super HG 100
Fujicolor Super HG 200
Fujicolor Super HG 400
Fujicolor Super HG 1600
Neopan 400 Professional
Neopan 1600

ILFORD, INC.
70 West Century Road
Paramus, New Jersey 07652
(201) 265-6000

Delta 400
Ilford FP4 Plus
Ilford HP5 Plus
Ilford Pan F
Ilford XP2 400

FUJI PHOTO FILM USA, INC.
555 Taxter Road
Elmsford, New York 10523
(914) 789-8100

Fujichrome 50
Fujichrome 50 Professional
Fujichrome 64T Professional
Fujichrome 100
Fujichrome 100 Professional D
Fujichrome 400
Fujichrome 400 Professional D

KONICA USA, INC.
440 Sylvan Avenue
Englewood Cliffs, New Jersey
07362
(201) 568-3100

Konica Color SR-G 160
Konica Super SR 100
Konica Super SR 200
Konica Super SR 400
Konica SR-G 3200

POLAROID CORPORATION
575 Technology Square
Cambridge, Massachusetts
 02139
(617) 577-2000

PolaBlue
Polachrome CS, HC
Polagraph HC
Polapan CT
Polaroid Onefilm
Spectra, 600 Plus
Time Zero Supercolor
Type 51
Types 52, 552 Polapan
Types 53, 553, 803 Black and
 White
Type 55 Positive/Negative
Type 87
Types 107, 084, 57
Types 107C, 667

Type 660 Polacolor EB
Types 661, 811
Types 664, 554, 54, 804
Type 665 Positive/Negative
Types 668, 58, 808
 Polacolor 2
Types 669, 108, 88, 59, 559,
 559 Silk, 809 Polacolor ER

3M COMPANY
3M Center Building
St. Paul, Minnesota 55144
(800) 695-FILM

ScotchChrome 100
ScotchChrome 400
ScotchChrome 640T
ScotchColor 100
ScotchColor 200
ScotchColor 400
ScotchChrome 1000